2⁴⁰

How To Read
ST. PAUL

Francois Amiot

How To Read
ST. PAUL

translated by

Michael D. Meilach O. F. M.

FRANCISCAN HERALD PRESS
Publishers of Franciscan Literature
Chicago, Illinois   60609

HOW TO READ ST. PAUL, translated into English by Michael Meilach O.F.M. from the French edition of Editions La Cordelle, 9 rue Marie-Rose, Paris XIVe, France, in the collection "Le Verbe Fait Chair," with the title *Lire Saint Paul*. Library of Congress Catalog Card Number: 64-24282, copyright 1964 by Franciscan Herald Press, 1434 West 51st Street, Chicago, Illinois 60609. Designed by Publication Associates. Made in the United States of America.

IMPRIMI POTEST
Donald Hoag O.F.M.
Minister Provincial, Holy Name Province

NIHIL OBSTAT
Mark Hegener O.F.M.
Censor Deputatus

IMPRIMATUR
Most Rev. Cletus F. O'Donnell, D.D.
Vicar General, Archdiocese of Chicago

August 27, 1964

TRANSLATOR'S PREFACE

Fr. Francois Amiot, a professor at the Séminaire de Saint-Sulpice, has made many contributions to contemporary biblical scholarship. Among his more important works are a commentary on the Letters to the Galatians and Thessalonians, a study of the Mass, a Life of Christ, and several articles for the French Encyclopedias *Catholicisme* and *Vocabulaire de théologie biblique*. His *Key Concepts of St. Paul*, published two years ago in English, has received a most enthusiastic welcome, and the French edition of this present work has sold over 50,000 copies in the first year of its publication.

It is a pleasure and a privilege, therefore, to present this English translation of *Lire Saint Paul*, which crystallizes the results of his long years of research on St. Paul. The work is, as he says in the Introduction, intended for the dedicated layman who has had no opportunity to engage in formal scripture studies. It is not a scientific study intended for theologians, but an eminently practical effort to present the timeless message of St. Paul to the modern apostles God has chosen to follow in the Saint's footsteps. Apparent on almost every page of this unpretentious but solidly doctrinal work, is the loving intimacy with St. Paul which the author has acquired by long years of patient, prayerful reflection on his subject.

This book is not for cursory scanning; it must be read

in the same spirit in which it was written: slowly, prayer-fully, and with a constant eye to the application in one's own spiritual life of the profound teachings it presents. The thought occurred to the translator many times, in the course of his work, that much of the book's impact might be lost if the reader did not take the time to read in full many of the verses of St. Paul which are here only referred to or quoted in part. This is why the footnotes have been printed on each page rather than relegated to the end of the book. They should be *used*; St. Paul should be given a chance to make his point fully at every turn, if the reader is to attain any real intimacy with the Apostle and his thought.

The translator and the publisher would like to thank the Bruce Publishing Company for permission to use the citations from the Kleist-Lilly translation of the New Testament, and the Confraternity of Christian Doctrine for the use of those which have been taken from its translation.

M.D.M.

St. Francis College
Rye Beach, New Hampshire
Feast of the Conversion of St. Paul
January 25, 1964.

CONTENTS

TRANSLATOR'S PREFACE 5

INTRODUCTION 9

Chapter One — ST. PAUL'S LETTERS 19
The General Structure of the Letters 19
The Characteristics of St. Paul's Language 21
Classification of the Letters 26

Chapter Two — ST. PAUL'S LITERARY
CHARACTERISTICS 29
St. Paul's Jewish and Greek Background 29
The Depth and Conciseness of St. Paul's Thought 30
St. Paul's Sensitivity 35
St. Paul's Imagination and the Comparisons He Uses .. 38
Antitheses: The Law and Faith, Flesh and Spirit, Adam
   and Christ 42
Personifications: Sin, Death, Life, and Grace 48
Other Peculiarities of St. Paul's Style 51
The "A,B,A'" Developments 56

Chapter Three — ST. PAUL'S DOCTRINE 61
The Doctrinal Significance of the Vision on the Way
   to Damascus 61
Justification through Faith 63
The Parousia 67
The Continuity of the Two Covenants; St. Paul's Use
   of Scripture 71
The Continuity between the Life of Grace and Eternal
   Life 75
Overall View of the Redemptive Plan 77

Chapter Four — ST. PAUL'S SPIRITUALITY 85
    The Divine Call and Its Demands 85
    Sharing in the Life of Christ Dead and Risen 87
    The Paschal Character of the Christian Life: The Eu-
        charist 91
    Trinitarian Spirituality 93
    A Spirituality of Love 98
    The Church, the Mystical Body of Christ 102
    Christian Morality 108
    Thanksgiving, Joy, and Peace 111
    The Eternal Perspective 114

BIBLIOGRAPHY 117

INTRODUCTION

This volume is addressed to the many Christians who attend Mass regularly but have not had the opportunity to engage in deeper scriptural studies. They have great respect for the Word of God dispensed to them in the course of the liturgical year; they would like to know it better so as to draw greater profit from it for their personal life as well as for the fecundity of the apostolate in which they participate. They need a guide, especially for St. Paul, and we would like to help those who read the Apostle by offering them some clarifications and advice.

The "Epistle" texts with which the use of the missal has familiarized every good parishioner cannot, because of their fragmentary character, give more than an incomplete knowledge of St. Paul. They contain some magnificent texts, some of which easily become a part of the reader and furnish him with valuable spiritual nourishment. One thinks, for example, of the Apostle's description of his work and his sufferings in the Epistle for Septuagesima Sunday;[1] or of the famous passage on Christ's humiliation and exaltation which the Church has us read on Palm Sunday.[2] But reading the excerpt at Mass is not enough; we must also study these passages in their own context. Some of them, in fact, are so shrouded in obscurity that they require ex-

1. 2 Cor. 11,19-12,9.
2. Phil. 2,5-11.

planations too extensive for any Sunday sermon. Most important of all, the interest and admiration awakened by the texts used in the Missal point to the need for an intimate acquaintance with the whole ensemble of St. Paul's writings.

Let us say, then, that a Christian has set out to do this— to undertake a systematic reading of all the Apostle's Letters, perhaps at the meetings of a biblical society, or even in quiet solitude, in those moments of leisure which he realizes he must put to good use to deepen his faith. The first thing he needs is a good translation; fortunately there have been many of these published which are commendable for their precision and, in many cases, their literary qualities as well.[3] If he knows Latin, he would do well to refer to the Vulgate text, which the priest reads at the altar and which faithfully follows the structure of the original Greek. The ideal would, of course, be to read St. Paul in Greek so as to lose none of the nuances of thought and expression that the most careful translations cannot render. Because of the unfortunate decline of classical studies, it is true, this ideal is rarely attainable. But anyone who has had the chance to study Greek will find it both enjoyable and profitable to read St. Paul in his own language. And this is true even though St. Paul used the "koine" Greek of conversation, commerce, and secular concerns in the first century of our era, which differs slightly from classical Greek.

Even the best prepared reader, however, will often find it difficult to understand St. Paul's teaching and to follow the thought he has so concisely expressed. Great minds— and St. Paul stands among the geniuses who have brought greatest honor to our race—are never easy to approach. Father Lagrange writes that when he began his renowned

_____
3. See the bibliography at the end of this book.

commentary on the Letter to the Romans, his first contact with it was overwhelming. But to be discouraged by this difficulty would be to deprive oneself of immeasurable spiritual benefit. If, on the other hand, one remains steadfast in his purpose—if he reads and re-reads Paul's Letters with the help of commentaries, careful reflection, and prayer — he will find ever new enlightenment both for himself and for the apostolic work which now more than ever is the duty of every Christian.

The primary requisites in understanding an author are (1) a knowledge of the circumstances in which he wrote and the aim he set for himself, and (2) a careful following of the development of his thought. In studying St. Paul, therefore, one should consult an introduction to the Letters, more or less detailed according to the time at his disposal. Then, without dwelling too long on that introduction, he should turn as soon as possible to the text itself. There will always be time later on, if it proves useful, to return to the introduction.[4] The reader will then do well to approach the Letters in their chronological order, which is not that found in our Bibles.[5] Their true chronology is reasonably certain now; the only real difficulties have to do with the dates of Galatians and Philippians, and the dates of these Letters are of little importance for an understanding of their teaching.[6]

It is also advisable to study St. Paul's Letters within the framework of the Acts of the Apostles, since the second part of that book is devoted exclusively to St. Paul by St.

4. Several introductions have been included in the bibliography, under the title "commentaries."
5. In the Bible, the Letters are arranged in order of decreasing size, those being placed last which are addressed to individuals: Timothy, Titus, and Philemon.
6. See the chronological table at the end of this introduction.

Luke, who was with him on some of his journeys. Correlating the Letters with the various chapters of Acts helps clarify many of their details and allusions; and it also shows that the Letters themselves were only one minor and occasional aspect of Paul's life-work. They are an important source for an understanding of that work, however, precisely because they are so closely bound up with it.

A first reading, made in the way just described, reveals St. Paul's preoccupations as he dictated his letters; it enables us to discern the broad outlines of his thought and to see how the difficulties he encountered in administering the churches led him to develop his thought and express it more exactly. Even at this stage, therefore, the reader will have gained a deep insight into the person of the Apostle and the main features of his doctrine.[7] He may find, though, that St. Paul does not present his principal ideas with the rigorous logical development he, the reader, would like to see. And that is true: St. Paul does in fact abound in digressions and unexpected parentheses which disconcert our western minds. What is more, the richness of his thought charges his words with explosive power; it dazzles us with intuitions which we admire but which make our heads swim because of their concentration. This is why we would advise, after a cursory first reading, the study of certain important passages grouped in a didactic order and thus adapted to our Cartesian mental habits.

This study will therefore begin with the major teachings of the Apostle but will on that account have the disadvantage of imposing upon St. Paul a logical framework which is not his own and which ignores the chronological order of his Letters, thus running the risk of misrepresent-

7. There are several repetitions in the chapters which follow, but these are unavoidable. St. Paul's texts are like diamonds which radiate light in many directions and must be viewed from all these angles if they are to be properly appreciated.

ing the circumstances and developments of St. Paul's thought. It will nevertheless be a useful procedure, for it will furnish a general view and serve as guide for a deeper reading to be done later in chronological order.

These are the passages we shall single out for explanation:

The divine plan of redemption: Eph. 1,3-14.

Christ and the election of the faithful: Rom. 1,1-7.

The mystery of Christ, God and man; Christ superior to the angels, head of the Church, Redeemer: Col. 1, 16-29.

Christ humbled and exalted: Phil. 2,5-11.

Christ, Son of God and superior to the angels: Heb. 1.

Adam and Christ: Rom. 5,12-21.

The two covenants; the Mosaic Law as teacher until Christ's coming: Gal. 4:1-7; Sara and Agar: Gal. 4,22-31; the letter and the spirit; the veil of Moses: 2 Cor. 3,5-18.

The priesthood of Christ: Heb. 4,14; 5,10.

Christ's sacrifice and its redemptive efficacy: Heb. 9,11-10,18.

The Redemption: gratuitous and universal justification through faith in Jesus Christ: Rom. 3,21-31; Gal. 3,15-21; Tit. 2,11-15; 3,4-8.

Baptism: Rom. 6,1-11; 22,23.

The justified man: Rom. 5,1-11.

The flesh and the spirit: Rom. 8,1-13.

Love: 1 Cor. 13.

The Eucharist: 1 Cor. 10,16-17; 11,23-34.

The hymn of Christian unity: Eph. 4,1-16.

The Work of the Holy Spirit in man; the future of the Christian: Rom. 8,14-39.

The interior man; earthly and heavenly dwelling: 2 Cor. 4,16-5, 10.

The Resurrection: 1 Cor. 15.

The Parousia: the mystery of iniquity and Antichrist: 2 Thess. 2,1-12; the glorious return of Christ and the fate of the last generation of Christians: 1 Thess. 4,12; 5,10; 1 Cor. 15,50-57.

A Chronology of St. Paul's Letters

32	or	33	— Conversion of St. Paul: Ac. 9,1-22.
32	—	35	— Stay at Damascus and Arabia: Gal. 1, 17.
		35	— Departure from Damascus, visit to Peter in Jerusalem, return to Tarsus: Ac. 9,23-30; Gal. 1,18-24.
		37	— St. Peter at Joppa and Caesarea: Ac. 9,31-11,18.
		43	— St. Paul at Antioch: Ac. 11,25-26.
		44	— Martyrdom of St. James the Greater: capture and deliverance of St. Peter: Ac. 12.
45	or	46	— Paul and Barnabas bring help to Jerusalem for an impending famine and then return to Antioch: Ac. 11, 29-30; Gal. 2,1-10.
46	(47)—	49	— First great journey of St. Paul with Barnabas: Cyprus and Asia Minor; return to Antioch: Ac. 13-14.
49			— The incident between Peter and Paul at Antioch: Gal. 2,11-21. *Letter to the Galatians?*
49	(50)		— Council of Jerusalem: Ac. 15,1-35.
50	—	52	— Second mission of St. Paul with Silas: Asia Minor, Macedonia, Athens, Corinth, return to Antioch: Ac. 15, 36-18,22.
51	—	52	— At Corinth, *The Letters to the Thes-*

				salonians. Arraignment before Gallio: Ac. 18,11-17.
53	—	57	(58) —	Third mission of St. Paul: Asia Minor. Ephesus, Corinth, Troas, Miletus, Jerusalem: Ac. 18,23-21,16. Between 53 and 56, at Ephesus, *Letter to the Galatians?*
Spring of 55 (56)			—	At Ephesus, *First Letter to the Corinthians* (1 Cor. 5,7-8).
56	or	57	—	In Macedonia, *Second Letter to the Corinthians; Letter to the Ephesians?*
57	or	58	—	At Corinth (Ac. 20,2; Rom. 16,1). *Letter to the Romans.* At Pentecost, arrest of St. Paul in Jerusalem: Ac. 21,17-23,30.
57 (58)—59 (60)			—	Imprisonment of St. Paul in Caesarea. Appeal to Caesar and transfer to Rome: Ac. 23,31-28,15.
60 (61)— 62(63)			—	First Roman Captivity (Ac. 28,16-31). *Letters to the Colossians, Ephesians, and Philippians?*
62	—	66	—	Liberation and last journeys of St. Paul: Spain (?), Crete, Asia Minor, Epirus, Achaia.
63	—	64	(or slightly later):	*Acts of the Apostles.*
64	—	66	—	*First Letter to Timothy, Letter to Titus.*
64	—			Martyrdom of St. Peter.
66			—	Second Roman Captivity of St. Paul; *Second Letter to Timothy.*
67			—	Martyrdom of St. Paul. *Letter to the Hebrews.*

How To Read
ST. PAUL

Chapter One

ST. PAUL'S LETTERS

The General Structure of the Letters

St. Paul's Letters, to begin with, are just that—letters. They are addressed to definite correspondents: either Christian communities or, in the case of the Pastoral Letters, individual followers of the Apostle. The circumstances of their composition are clearly reflected in their content. The Letter to the Galatians, e.g., was prompted by the Jewish converts' presumption in trying to make circumcision and the practices of the Mosaic Law obligatory for Christians of pagan origin. St. Paul expresses himself vehemently in this Letter, for by imposing the Law on pagans as a condition for their conversion, the Judaizers had held up the progress of the gospel. He was certain, moreover, that since Christ had abolished the Law by his redemptive death, it could no longer be considered in any way a condition for salvation. The First Letter to the Corinthians answers a series of conscience cases raised by the faithful and opposes the abuses introduced in the Corinthian community. The Letters to the Colossians and Ephesians refute errors concerning the person of Christ. The Pastoral Letters give Timothy and Titus directions for the government of their churches.

As was customary in ancient times, the Letters begin with a salutation in which St. Paul addresses to his correspondents a prayer, almost always the same, which combines and "baptizes" the standard Greek and Hebrew salutations: "Grace be to you and peace from God our Father and our Lord Jesus Christ." There ordinarily follow some friendly words to the addressees: the Apostle assures them of a remembrance in his prayers, and his apostolic concern and spiritual fatherliness here find touching expression.

The body of the Letter usually contains two parts, the first doctrinal and the second exhortatory; they are generally referred to as the "dogmatic" and "moral" sections. This division must be understood with some flexibility, however; it is particularly valid for the Letters to the Romans, the Galatians, the Colossians, and the Ephesians, but not in such a way that St. Paul can be said to impose rigid artificial structures on his style. The Letters to the Thessalonians and to the Philippians have a more informal style; in these cases St. Paul expresses himself freely and, especially in Philippians, is bound by no rigorous plan. On the other hand, the first eleven chapters of the Letter to the Romans form an orderly and elegant exposition of the redemptive plan and the sharing by the faithful in the salvation brought by Christ. The same is true of the first three chapters of Ephesians, and a similar observation can be made with regard to the first part of the Letter to the Hebrews, the editing of which, however, is due to one of the Apostle's followers.

The Letters end with brief exhortations without any definite order, often followed by greetings to Christians known to Paul; they take up practically the whole last chapter of the Letter to the Romans. To close his Letters, the Apostle uses a prayer which varies in expression but whose general theme expresses a thought dear to him: "May the grace of our Lord Jesus Christ be with you." And then it occurs to him to take the pen from his secretary's hand and write a few words (in capital letters): "See with

what large letters I write to you with my own hand!"[1] In
one Letter, he specifies that this signed salutation is a proof
of the Letter's authenticity—a necessary precaution, since
some false letters seem to have been circulated under his
name:[2] "This greeting is in my own hand—Paul's the signa-
ture in every letter of mine. This is my handwriting. The
grace of our Lord Jesus Christ be with you all!"[3]

Then the Letter is closed, sealed, and entrusted to a
safe courier. One or another seems to have been copied
several times before being dispatched; this is probably the
case with the Letter to the Ephesians, which is apparently
a circular letter meant for the churches of Asia Minor.

The Characteristics of St. Paul's Language

Following the custom of his time, St. Paul dictated his
Letters, and it is possible that he even gave his secretary
some latitude in expressing his thought. This is generally
enough admitted for the Letters of the Captivity and the
Pastoral Letters. But it is not accepted by everyone, for
St. Paul's genius was extremely rich and at times made
use of unexpected expressions, examples of which can be
found in all his Letters, including those whose editing in-
terpreters have declined to attribute to him. This has lent
weight to the position of those who claim that the Letters
are all authentically Pauline.[4]

St. Paul's lively temperament, so characteristically oriental, never shrank from verbal excesses or paradoxes.
These modes of expression must be well understood and,

1. Gal. 6, 11.
2. 2 Thess. 2,2.
3. 2 Thess. 3,17-18.
4. Many passages of the Pastoral Letters (1 Tim. 3,16;
   6,12-16; Tit. 2,11-14; 3,4-6; 2 Tim. 1,9-11; 2,8-10; etc.)
   have a clearly Pauline character.

if one may put it thus, not taken too seriously. The preaching of the Cross is nonsense, but only for those who are
on the road to destruction; it is the power of God for those
who are on the road to salvation.[5] For this reason, God
has "turned to nonsense the wisdom of this world, "[6] i.e.,
the abuse of a philosophy at once superficial and ration-
alistic before the letter. Such a "philosophy" is closed to
the light of divine revelation, but not so with the right
use of reason. St. Paul expects men to infer from the spectacle of creation the existence of God, "especially his everlasting power and divinity."[7] Again, Christ "became the object of a curse"[8] to redeem us—became sin personified, so to
speak. This means that on the Cross he took on himself the
curses of the Law and all our sins to deliver us from them.

The weaker the Apostle seems, the stronger he is;[9] the
world considers as deceivers those who preach the gospel,
whereas they are truthful; it considers them to be at death's
door, whereas they continue to live; it thinks they have
nothing, whereas they possess everything.[10] Paul makes himself a Jew to the Jews; and to those not having the Law,
a man not having the Law.[11] He overflows with joy in spite
of all his troubles, and he considers himself nailed, with
Christ, to the Cross.[12] Jesus emptied himself for us by taking
the nature of a slave and became obedient to death on a
cross.[13] All these paradoxes, however, add up to the supreme

---

5. 1 Cor. 1,18.
6. 1 Cor. 1,20.
7. Rom. 1,19-20.
8. Gal. 3,13; cf. 2 Cor. 5,21, where the Greek and the Vulgate say
   that Christ "was made sin."
9. 2 Cor. 12,10.
10. 2 Cor. 6,8-10.
11. 1 Cor. 9,19-22.
12. 2 Cor. 7,4; Gal. 2,20.
13. Phil. 2,7-8.

paradox of redemption through the Cross and sharing its fruits in union with Jesus dead and risen. The excited subtlety of the reasoning is therefore only apparent, and the difficulties vanish when we have come by long acquaintance to know the Apostle.

Nor must we take Paul's ironies too literally, as, e.g., when he urges the Thessalonians, who no longer wish to work because they consider our Lord's return imminent, not to eat.[14] Irony abounds in the Corinthian Letters. Paul rejoices that in the church at Corinth there are above all men whom the world considers foolish, and few of noble birth.[15] He can give the Corinthians only basic spiritual food comparable to milk, because they are still children and not yet adults in Christ.[16] And he chides with a paternally malicious gentleness their naive pretention to be "something," whereas the Apostles, with whom they claim kinship, are vagabonds, doomed to death, called ugly names, and rejected as the world's scum.[17]

Throughout his entire Second Letter to the Corinthians, Paul reproaches with exquisite irony those who contradict his authority: super-apostles, he calls them, who take the limelight on every possible occasion and with whom he declares that he will not have the audacity to class himself or even to compare himself.[18] Then he proceeds to put them in their place and write a magnificent panegyric to himself, to which their subterfuges have driven him.[19]

Another rhetorical device attributable to the Apostle's vivacity is *analogia personae*, whereby he places himself at

14. 2 Thess. 3,10.
15. 1 Cor. 1,26-27.
16. 1 Cor. 3,1-3.
17. 1 Cor. 4,8-16.
18. 2 Cor. 11,5; 10,12.
19. 2 Cor. 11,16-12,13.

the other person's viewpoint. Thus he speaks in the first person of "we who are alive" at the time of Christ's return, and then adopts the contrary hypothesis only a few lines later.[20] Similarly, he declares in another Letter that "just as God raised the Lord, so he will raise us by his power," supposing that he will be dead at the time of the Parousia. But, in the ignorance we all share regarding the time of the last day, which allows for its possible imminence, he says a few chapters later that "we shall not all fall asleep in death, but we shall all be changed.[21]

All this goes to show, in passing, how ill those have understood St. Paul who have attributed to him the conviction that he would live until Christ's second coming.[22] The same procedure is apparent in the lament of the Letter to the Romans, where the Apostle uses a fictitious "I" to express the drama of man in the grips of sin to which he is as it were sold, doing what he would not and hating what he does, until he has understood that Christ alone can give him victory over the Law, over Sin and Death.[23]

Since the Letters are evidently circumstantial writings, it is hardly surprising that the same Letter deals with various subjects in a way adapted to the needs of its addressees, or that it sometimes treats these matters in a summary and one-sided manner which may seem to contradict the Apostle's true thought. One who were to read only the Letter to the Galatians could be led to believe that the Mosaic Law was primarily intended to increase the sinner's misery by multiplying the disobediences made possible by its precepts.[24] But the Letter to the Romans shows that the

20. Thess. 4,15-17; 5,5-10.
21. 1 Cor. 6,4; 15,51.
22. See below, pp. 67-70.
23. Rom. 7,7-25.
24. Gal. 3,19-22.

Law is good, just, and holy;[25] that it embodies a lofty ideal to which man could conform if he had faith in the messianic promises and sought God's help.

Marriage, relegated to second place in the First Corinthian Letter, by comparison to the virginal state, is raised in Ephesians to an incomparable dignity when the Apostle compares the union of the spouses to that of Christ and the Church.[26] In Romans, and elsewhere as well, Paul sometimes seems to say that men are predestined, whatever they do, some to salvation and others to damnation. God "has mercy on whom he pleases, and he hardens whom he pleases."[27] Yet man's freedom and responsibility in accepting or rejecting the gospel message are constantly affirmed: no one is damned except through his own fault. We must not let Paul's insistence on God's sovereign liberty in his choice and his gifts (an insistence which had also pervaded the Old Testament) obscure his equally emphatic teaching that the divine initiative always respects human liberty.

We must therefore bear in mind the entire doctrinal context of Paul's Letters and correlate his varying viewpoints; then we shall be amazed by the depth and coherence of his teaching. We shall find that the elements of that teaching, despite their episodic character, form a virtually complete body of doctrine, a precious gift from God to his Church and a treasure from which she will never cease to draw new life. It is not surprising, in view of these facts, that some allusions remain obscure. We do not understand the baptism "for the dead," for example;[28] and we have not yet managed to identify clearly the errors condemned by the Letters of the Captivity and the Pastoral Letters. But these

25. Rom. 7,12-14.
26. 1 Cor. 7; Eph 5,22-33.
27. Rom. 9,18.
28. 1 Cor. 15,29.

points are of only secondary importance. They are insignificant difficulties which in no way mar our understanding of the doctrinal ensemble or synthesis set forth in the "theologies" of St. Paul.[29]

The eloquent and impassioned character of the Pauline Letters reveals a rapid dictation. The thought broadens at times into so impetuous a torrent that the sentence is left unfinished,[30] and, according to several Latin authors, the secretaries were hard put to get the words down on paper. It is difficult to escape the impression that St. Paul formulated his thought with a rapid spontaneity whose inspiration a slow secretary often interrupted.[31]

Classification of the Letters

Several attempts have been made to classify St. Paul's Letters. The one given below is the most common, but it is still somewhat arbitrary. It is furnished here merely for convenience.

(1) The Great Letters: Romans, 1 and 2 Corinthians, Galatians;

(2) The Letters of the First Captivity: Ephesians, Philippians, and Colossians—also called the Christological Letters because of their teachings on the person and transcendence of Christ—to which should be added the note to Philemon; and

(3) The Pastoral Letters: 1 and 2 Timothy and Titus, addressed to the Apostle's followers whom he had

---

29. See bibliography.
30. E.g., in 2 Cor 5,7; Rom. 5,12; 9,22-24; Eph. 2,2; 3,1; etc.; see F. Prat, S.J., *The Theology of St. Paul* (see bibliography), vol. 1, p. 69.
31. F. Brunot, *Le genie litteraire de saint Paul* (Paris: Editions du Cerf), p. 202, says that St. Paul probably took between seven and ten hours to dictate his Letters to the Romans.

placed in charge of churches—in these the doctrinal character is less evident.

The Letter to the Hebrews is placed in a separate category; it was edited by a follower of St. Paul whose identity is unknown. Although his thought is certainly Pauline, this writer uses too unique a style for his role to be reduced to that of a secretary.

Chapter Two

ST. PAUL'S LITERARY CHARACTERISTICS

St. Paul's Jewish and Greek Background

St. Paul had the advantage of a twofold formation, Jewish and Greek. Like every young Jew, he had begun even in his earliest childhood to read the Bible with earnest devotion, and later on, in Jerusalem, he had studied under the renowned Gamaliel.[1] It was under this scholar's direction that the young Saul acquired his outstanding knowledge of the Bible, so evident in the many allusions and citations found in his Letters. His familiarity with the inspired Word gave him a religious depth, a sense of God's grandeur and activity in history which contributed greatly to his understanding of the redemptive plan. At the same time, the Bible furnished him with a rich treasure of images, a taste for hyperbole, antithesis, comparison, and certain types of reasoning characteristic of the oriental genius. The general tone of his Letters—there is hardly need to verify this—is redolent of Old Testament writing. Even in our own day, Jewish converts step firmly and easily into the satisfying atmosphere of the New Testament, where they meet once more the ways of thought and language which are so familiar to them. They are delighted to find that their sacred books receive in the New Testament a crown in perfect continuity with the faith of Israel.

1. Ac. 22,23.

29

But besides being an accomplished rabbi, St. Paul was also a Greek who read Scripture in the Septuagint Greek as well as in the Hebrew text. Both before and after his conversion, he lived in a predominantly Greek environment. He was heir to Hellenism's great richness of vocabulary, its fine delicacy of thought and expression (which so well complemented the more concrete style of the Semitic genius), and its taste for dialectic. He loved to argue and would delight in sparring with an imaginary opponent—putting to good use the subtle methods of the Stoic philosophers. His style thus has a vivacity which is far more convincing than cold, abstract, syllogistic reasoning. Read, for example, the simulated dialogues on the abrogation of the Mosaic Law and on salvation through faith in Jesus Christ. Chapters 2, 3, and 9 of Romans, in particular, are made up of dialogues which exclude every subterfuge and leave the reader stunned, if not convinced, by the liveliness and rigor of their reasoning.

Thus had our Lord prepared for himself, in St. Paul, a chosen instrument to carry his name to the whole world[2] and endowed him with qualities rarely combined to such a degree: a powerful intelligence and a deep sensitivity.

The Depth and Conciseness of St. Paul's Thought

The Apostle's mind was extraordinarily penetrating and profound. Besides being a logician, he had an intuitive faculty which leapt in one step from basic principles to their ultimate consequences, without always showing his readers the intermediate premises of his reasoning. He also had a way of expressing an important point with extreme brevity. This is true especially in the great doctrinal Letters such as Romans, Galatians, and Ephesians, but the same phe-

2. Ac. 9,15.

nomenon can be found throughout his writings. Without any warning, sometimes, even in the midst of a moral exhortation, he will suddenly develop a dogmatic point just as deeply as in any of the major Letters. This is the case in the famous passage of Philippians on Christ's abasement and exaltation;[3] it is true in his First Letter to Timothy where he speaks of the "mystery of the true religion";[4] it is true in the Letter to Titus with reference to the Redemption and baptismal rebirth.[5] This rapid passing from primary intuitions to ultimate conclusions is evidently traceable to the vision which converted the persecuting Pharisee and showed him in an all-revealing flash that Jesus of Nazareth was the awaited Messia, that his Resurrection authenticated his teachings and that he was the true and unique Savior. Paul was thus placed at one stroke in full possession of what he loved to call his gospel, or the gospel of Christ.[6] He realized, consequently, that the Mosaic Law had been powerless to justify and was definitively abolished, that only faith in Christ could assure man of salvation.

Some passages in his Letters, in fact, clearly reveal the influence of that episode on the way to Damascus. Writing to the Galatians, for example, he says:

> Yet we know that no man is sanctified by the deeds the Law prescribes, but by faith in Jesus Christ. Hence we believe in Christ Jesus, that we may be sanctified with faith in Christ Jesus as the starting point, and not by the deeds the Law prescribes, because by such legal deeds no man is sanctified .... As for me, by the law of faith I have died to the Law that I may live for God. With Christ I am nailed

3. Phil. 2,5-11.
4. 1 Tim. 3,16
5. Tit. 2,13-14; 3,4-7. The similarity between all these passages is an argument in favor of the authencity of the Pastoral Letters.
6. Gal. 1,7,9,11; Rom. 2,16.

to the cross. It is now no longer I who live, but Christ lives in me.[7]

To grasp this line of reasoning, one must first know that the man who believes in Christ is united, through baptism, to his redemptive death, and that this mystical death has freed him forever from the Law. But Paul does not spell out these truths, and we can understand the passage only by complementing it with the teaching found in the Letter to the Romans.

Other equally concise expressions contain a whole world of ideas. "You know, in fact, the graciousness of our Lord Jesus Christ. Although he was rich, he became poor for your sakes that by his poverty you might become rich."[8] "For if you confess with your lips that Jesus is the Lord, and believe in your heart that God raised him from the dead, you shall be saved."[9] God has revealed to us "the mystery of his will. And this good pleasure he decreed to put into effect in Christ when the designated period of time had elapsed, namely to gather all creation both in heaven and on earth under one head, Christ."[10] "No longer is there Jew or Greek; no longer is there slave or freeman; no longer is there male or female. You are all one in Christ Jesus."[11] "You are Christ's body and individually its members."[12]

These texts are such that meditation on them never ceases to unearth new riches. But their compact and elliptical style requires that they be replaced within the whole framework of the Apostle's teaching, which is centered on redemption through the blood of Christ. The fruit of the

7. Gal. 2,16, 19-20.
8. 2 Cor. 8,9.
9. Rom. 10,9.
10. Eph. 1,9-10.
11. Gal. 3,28.
12. 1 Cor. 12,27.

Redemption is a sharing in Christ's life, a union of all believers with Christ and with one another in the unity of a unique body of which they become the members and of which Christ is the head. One must return to these basic intuitions which dominate and explain the Apostle's thought if he is to grasp the full meaning and import of the striking texts whose brevity makes them so difficult to interpret.

Often the Apostle meets a difficulty with a concise answer which goes to the heart of the matter and makes any reply impossible. For example, the moving passage of the Letter to the Galatians cited above (on justification through faith in Jesus Christ and the abrogation of the Mosaic Law) ends with this crushing argument: "If holiness comes by the Law, then Christ's death is to no purpose."[13] The absurdity of the conclusion proves the falsity of the premise.

At Corinth, the faithful had begun to form little cliques which claimed their origin, one from Paul, another from his follower Apollos, another from Peter, and a fourth from Christ himself, whose teaching it pretended to possess more perfectly. The Apostle makes short work of these attempts to undermine the unity of the Church: "Is Christ at war with himself?"[14] Then he deftly places his own authority in proper perspective as well, reproaching those who have become inordinately attached to him: "Was Paul crucified for you? Or were you baptized in the name of Paul?"

For the noblest motives, yet with the most forceful judgment, he exhorts these same Corinthians (perhaps not fully weaned from their tawdry past) to forsake impurity:

Are you not aware that your bodies are members of Christ's

13. Gal. 2,21.
14. 1 Cor. 1,13.

body? Shall I then take the members of Christ and make them the members of a prostitute? Never! Are you not aware that your body is the temple of the Holy Spirit? Him you have received from God! You are not your own masters. You have been bought, and at a price! So then, glorify God in your body.[15]

The question of meat offered to idols is treated with similar loftiness of vision. In itself, the use of this food is indifferent, since idols are nothing. But one must respect the scruples of Christians as yet ill-enlightened and avoid scandalizing them: "By your knowledge he is destroyed, this brother for whose sake Christ died! When you so sin against your brothers, and wound their weak conscience, it is against Christ that you sin."[16]

Some years later, the Apostle exhorted the Corinthians to take up a generous collection for the impoverished Church at Jerusalem. It was only right that they help with their material alms those from whom they had received so great spiritual benefits. So Paul insists with delicate tact. He gives no order, but uses an unexpected argument whose depth anticipates the great text of Philippians: "You know, in fact, the graciousness of our Lord Jesus Christ. Although he was rich, he became poor for your sakes that by his poverty you might become rich."[17] How can one not be convinced by such an example?

Many other instances can be found in Paul's Letters which are just as salient, just as rich. The Apostle's orders and advice are always fortified with some motive based on the profound doctrinal insights which never ceased to enliven his spirit.

15. 1 Cor. 6,15, 19-20.
16. 1 Cor. 8,11-12.
17. 2 Cor. 8,9.

St. Paul's Sensitivity

The many striking expressions found in St. Paul's Letters bespeak a quivering sensitivity and a heart of fire whose irresistible power has won innumerable believers for Christ. The Apostle's spirit and character shines through in his letters to a degree which is doubtless unmatched by any other writer.

His sensitivity is immediately apparent, for example, at the beginning of the Letter to the Galatians, where he takes his correspondents to task with extreme intensity, accusing them of letting the true gospel be perverted by Judaizers who presumed to impose on them the Mosaic Law and circumcision:

> I am astounded that for another gospel you are so quickly deserting him, who, thanks to the grace of Christ, has called you. There is no other gospel; it is merely that some people are upsetting you and wish to distort the gospel of Christ. Let me tell you that if even we ourselves or an angel from heaven should proclaim to you a gospel other than we have proclaimed, let him be accursed.[18]

There then follows a closely woven argument in which Paul defends the authenticity of his mission and shows the agreement of his teaching with that of Peter and the other Apostles, and in the course of which he adds many another deadly thrust at the foolish Galatians who have allowed themselves to be so "bewitched."[19] But he loves them deeply, and his heart wins the day with this moving admission:

> My dear children, I am again suffering the pangs of childbirth for you, until Christ is formed within you. Yet I wish I could be with you at the present moment, and thus adjust

18. Gal. 1,6-8.
19. Gal. 3,1.

my words to the situation, because I do not know what to make of you.[20]

This is typical of Paul's attitude; he is always overflowing with an utterly tender love for those whom he has won for Christ. Writing to the Thessalonians, he compares himself to a nursing mother fondling her children, and to a father entreating, encouraging, and adjuring his children. He is ready to give his life for them, so dear have they become to him.[21] Yet his affection is not blind, and he has some severe reproaches for those "enlightened ones" who refused to work under the pretext that the Savior's glorious return was imminent.[22]

The First Letter to the church at Corinth likewise combines peremptory advice and justified severity with protestations of fatherly love.[23] The gravest sanctions Paul is forced to impose—e.g., with regard to an incestuous man—are intended only for the amendment and eventual salvation of the guilty parties.[24] The most striking example of this variety of tone and emotion is found in the Second Letter to this same church, throughout the whole of which the Apostle is forced to defend himself against his implacable opponents — "super-apostles," he ironically calls them[25] — who misrepresent his intentions and usurp his authority. Read this extraordinary defense in which every emotion is brought to bear and which ends with the striking description of Paul's apostolic labors; never has a man bared his heart with such richness, penetration, and religious depth. The reproaches occasionally exceed moderation, but how

20. Gal. 4,19-20.
21. 1 Thess. 2,8-11.
22. 2 Thess. 3,6-12.
23. 1 Cor. 3,14-15.
24. 1 Cor. 5,1-5.
25. 2 Cor. 11,5.

easily we forgive the Apostle for them, since his faithfulness to his mission and his love shine forth throughout!

With the Philippians, toward whom he bore an especial love because of their tenderness toward him, the tone is more calm, and Paul expresses himself with loving abandon.[26] The same affectionate fatherliness is evident in the Pastoral Letters where he lavishes his advice on his beloved followers whom he has appointed as heads of churches.[27] In the note to Philemon, he becomes ingratiating; with exquisite tenderness he begs pardon for a fugitive slave whom he sends back as a convert, having begotten him while in chains, and asks his master to receive him kindly and henceforth treat him as a beloved brother.[28]

Even in the solemn doctrinal discourses addressed to the Romans, Paul reveals the kindness of his heart. He is saddened, for example, by the unbelief of his brothers in Israel, to the point of wishing to be anathema, forever separated from Christ, if only that could assure their salvation.[29] But our admiration for Paul reaches new heights when we realize the extent to which his immeasurable love for his "children" is rooted in the love of Christ himself: "I live by faith in the Son of God, who loved me and sacrificed himself for me."[30] Paul's whole heart is in this unforgettable cry. His whole life is one of constant intimacy with Jesus Christ, whom our heavenly Father has wished to make the first-born among many brothers and whose love has led him to deliver himself for us.[31]

"Who shall separate us from Christ's love for us? . . .

26. Phil. 4,10-20.
27. 2 Tim. 1,4; 4,9, etc.
28. Philem. 10-15.
29. Rom. 9,1-5.
30. Gal. 2,20.
31. Rom. 8,29; Eph. 5,2.

[No] creature can separate us from God's love for us, which is in Christ Jesus our Lord."[32] As has rightly been observed, Paul's heart is Christ's heart. Out of love for his Master and for the faithful, who are members of his body and one with him,[33] he makes himself "everybody's slave to win the more converts."[34] Such lofty aspirations as these give us the key to St. Paul's vibrant sensitivity. They explain his unceasing, restless concern for those he has brought to spiritual life. They explain his excesses, his frequent and ardent outbursts. They explain everything.

St. Paul's Imagination and the Comparisons He Uses

Paul's sensitivity was enhanced by a rich imagination and a passionate temperament. These qualities, which enabled him to feel everything keenly, also helped him to put across the Christian teachings so well formulated by his magnificent mind. That is why we find, all through his Letters, an extremely personal tone and an eloquence so much the more appealing as it is selfless and artless. His innermost feelings shine forth everywhere and give all his writings an inimitable character. Anyone who reads St. Paul feels his extraordinary power and, if he is sincerely converted to God, reaps great benefit from it. In this respect the Apostle is the forefather of a distinguished line of writers which has contributed immeasurably to the Church's life and which includes among its illustrious members St. Augustine, St. Teresa, Pascal, and Cardinal Newman.

Contrary to what we might expect, in light of St. Paul's extensive travels, he seems to have been little impressed

32. Rom. 8,35,38.
33. 1 Cor. 12,27; Gal. 3,28.
34. 1 Cor. 9,19-22.

by the spectacle of nature or by the places he visited on his journeys. He was of urban origin and exercised his apostolic ministry almost exclusively in cities, from which the gospel could most easily be spread. His attention was attracted mainly to interior realities: the gift of faith, the communication of the redemptive mystery, and the transformation of men's hearts by Christ, the object of his constant wonder. Thus the images he uses are borrowed especially from psychology and human activity.

The best known of these comparisons is that of the human body. The faithful are members of one immense organism, the body of Christ, in which each one has his function and contributes to the good of the whole in a solidarity at once deeper and more effective than the one which joins together the various parts of the human body.[35] Christ communicates his life to each of his members and unites them most intimately to himself. The comparison is completed and made more precise in the Letters of the Captivity, where we find Christ portrayed as the head of this vast supernatural organism; he is the source of life, of authority, and of coherence, although he also seems to be the whole body, which has life only through him.[36] But this body of Christ, which he quickens, is also his Church. As such, it manifests his life outwardly[37] in two ways: first, by the participation of each member and of the whole body in the one Spirit; and second, by the eating of the Savior's glorified Body in the Eucharist.[38] This Pauline teaching on the body of Christ—the "mystical body," as theologians call it—has been considerably developed and deepened in our

35. 1 Cor. 12,12-30.
36. Col. 2,19; 3,15; Eph. 3,6; 4,4,15.
37. Col. 2,24; Eph. 1,22-23.
38. 1 Cor. 10,16-17.

own time; its implications become more and more apparent with the passage of time.[39]

The comparison of the body is somewhat similar to that of the building, and so St. Paul occasionally combined the two.[40] According to this latter analogy, Christ is the cornerstone of a spiritual edifice whose foundation is formed by the Apostles and Prophets. It is from Christ that the building derives solidity, coherence, growth, and holiness.[41] By their apostolic work, Christians build on the unique foundation with material of uneven quality. On Judgment Day God will give a just appraisal of this material. The Apostles are, after all, only his collaborators, and he alone gives the increase.[42] The faithful thus form the temple of God, an abode of the Holy Spirit worthy of the deepest respect.[43] Paul dwells constantly on the relations between the Christian and the divine Persons who dwell in him.[44] Indeed, for him this Indwelling, made possible by Christ's redeeming blood, constitutes an essential aspect of the Christian life.

These comparisons bring out clearly the spiritual intimacy and the unity which characterize our life in Christ. Another favorite image of Paul's, that of the conjugal union, is equally forceful. The point of this figure is that the faithful are wedded to a unique Spouse; they are like a pure virgin presented to Christ.[45] The loving union between the Church and Christ, who gave his life for her, is thus presented by the Apostle as a perennial model for the union

39. Even at this point we can glimpse the moral consequences St. Paul deduced from this doctrine; see below, pp. 108-11.
40. 1 Cor. 6,19-20; Eph. 4,16.
41. Eph. 2,19-22.
42. 1 Cor. 3,5-15; 4,1-2.
43. 1 Cor. 3,16-17; 6,19-20.
44. Rom. 8,11; Eph. 3,17; etc.
45. 2 Cor. 11,2.

of Christian spouses in love and mutual respect.[46] This is
an old and eminently biblical comparison, from which Paul
draws a profound lesson, while at the same time raising
to an unparalleled dignity the sacrament of Christian marriage.

St. Paul uses still other comparisons to illustrate the
teaching and exhortations of his Letters. He urges the
Christian to work for an imperishable crown with at least
as much spirit of sacrifice and courage as track athletes
bring to their work. Indeed, athletic contests promise only
a perishable crown given to one man, whereas in the Christian spiritual life all can and should gain the prize.[47] The
Christian, moreover, is well armed in this difficult struggle;
he has at his disposal a veritable spiritual arsenal: truth,
justice, faith, and the hope of salvation—which St. Paul
engagingly likens to the various pieces of armament worn
by the Roman soldier.[48]

Recalling that he was a tentmaker, Paul encourages the
Corinthians by speaking to them of the everlasting tent,
not made by human hands, which is reserved for them in
heaven and which, undaunted by the mixed metaphor, he
likens to a garment. We should wish to don this garment
over our earthly clothes, he continues, if only we could go
to Christ without first passing through death.[49]

Those who work to spread the gospel are like gardeners
who plant and water.[50] The Israelites (who the Apostle fore-
sees will one day come to Christ) are like branches cut off
the olive tree to which they belong. But they can be re-
grafted more easily than the wild branches which stand for

46. Eph. 5,22-33.
47. 1 Cor. 9,24-27.
48. Eph. 6,13-17.
49. 2 Cor. 5,1-4.
50. 1 Cor. 3,6.

the pagans, converted in great numbers despite the difficulties involved in their insertion into the true olive tree.[51]

Just as the first-fruits herald the coming harvest, so Christ's Resurrection is a pledge of our own;[52] and our Savior, the Paschal Lamb who was sacrificed for us, invites us to celebrate the new Pasch, "not with the old yeast, the yeast of malice and wickedness, but with the unleavened bread of sincerity and integrity."[53]

The abundance of images and comparisons in St. Paul is, then, apparent. But, except for the digression on the mystical body in the First Letter to the Corinthians,[54] they are for the most part briefly stated. They are only a support for Paul's thought and are not developed like the gospel parables. It would be tedious to list them all here, but we shall call attention to some others as we discuss further peculiarities of the Apostle's style.

Antitheses: The Law and Faith, Flesh and Spirit, Adam and Christ

Paul's sudden conversion occasioned by his vision of Christ, and his resulting assurance of the redemption and renewal of the universe by the sacrifice of Calvary led him to engage in a continual game of antitheses—a procedure relished by Jews and Greeks alike—in which he opposed the New Covenant to the Old, the state of the reborn Christian to that of sinful man: "If, then, any man is in Christ he is a new creation; the old state of things has gone; wonderful to tell, it has been made over, absolutely new!"[55]

51. Rom. 11,17-24.
52. 1 Cor. 15,20-23.
53. 1 Cor. 5,6-8.
54. 1 Cor. 12.
55. 2 Cor. 5,17.

The reign of faith has replaced that of the Mosaic Law. The Letters to the Galatians and the Romans show at great length and with many a complicated digression (which should not be too surprising, considering the complexity of the subject), that the Mosaic Law was abolished by Christ's sacrifice. Of itself, it had never been able to justify the Jew; it simply laid down, like any legislative norm, prescriptions which it could not empower him to observe. The power needed had to be sought in God's help, through faith in the fulfillment of the messianic promises. This provisional economy has now been abolished; the faith which justifies is now faith in Christ, in whom all the promises have found their fulfillment. The position of the Jewish converts who presumed to impose the observance of the Law as a condition for salvation[56] led St. Paul to react vigorously and to crystallize the opposition between the two successive economies in his celebrated "Law-Faith" antitheses.

Another antithesis exploited by the Apostle is that of "Flesh-Spirit." Ordinarily he understands by the term "flesh" not merely material flesh, but the whole framework of man's tendency toward sin.[57] In this sense even knowledge can be called carnal[58] and St. Paul can list among the most loathsome works of the flesh those disorders which in reality stem from the soul: idolatry, enmities, discord, along with fleshly sins properly so-called.[59] This is a legitimate way of speaking, based on the relations between soul and body which St. Paul so clearly perceived. It is particularly justified by the fact that the tendency to sin finds in the flesh its most obvious, if not its most formidable, manifestations. The flesh thus becomes synonymous with weakness, imper-

56. Ac. 15,1.
57. Rom. 8,7.
58. Col. 2,18, Vg.
59. Gal. 5,19-21.

fection, corruptibility; and these various meanings are often combined.

> For what was impossible to the Law, in that it was weak because of the flesh [as source of sin], God has made good. By sending his Son in the likeness of sinful flesh [a human nature subject to suffering and death] as a sin-offering [i.e., to overcome sin], has condemned sin in the flesh [the very flesh of Christ and of mankind united to him by faith in him], in order that the requirements of the Law might be fulfilled in us, who walk not according to the flesh, but according to the spirit.[60]

The term "spirit" signifies, besides the higher part of the soul, the whole ensemble of good tendencies inspired by the Holy Spirit. Just as the sinful soul can be called carnal, so the body consecrated to God's service becomes, in a sense, spirit, even as it awaits the incorruptibility and "spiritualization" it will receive at the general resurrection.[61] (This is not to say, of course, that it will become immaterial, but only that it will be fully subject to the soul.)

In the final analysis, "the spirit" designates man under the influence of the Holy Spirit; and "the flesh," man deprived of that influence. The opposition between flesh and spirit in this sense is thus seen to be irreducible; every man must choose between the tendencies of the flesh, which lead to hatred of God, and those of the spirit, subject to the Law of God.[62] From this it follows that the term "spirit" can connote three things: the Holy Spirit, a divine Person; the merely natural, spiritual part of man; and this same spiritual part of man as supernaturalized by the Spirit's presence and action:

60. Rom. 8,3-4, Conf.
61. 1 Cor. 15,42-44.
62. Rom. 8,5-8.

You, however, are not sensual but spiritual [the spirit of man transformed by the Spirit of God], if the Spirit of God [the divine Person] really dwells in you, whereas no one who is deprived of the Spirit of Christ belongs to Christ. But if Christ is in you, the body, it is true, is destined for death because of sin; but the spirit [the spirit of supernaturalized man] has life because of its holiness. . . . The Spirit himself joins his testimony to that of our spirit [the spirit of the man he quickens] that we are children of God.[63]

The meaning of these terms, as is true of so many others in the Pauline Letters, must therefore be determined from the context in which they are used. This is one of the difficulties inherent in Paul's style and at the same time an indication of its richness.

The flesh and the spirit, as St. Paul understands them, lead respectively to "death" and to "life." Here again, the breadth of meaning contained in two antithetical terms is remarkable. "Death" is at the same time spiritual death (sin), bodily death (its consequence), and eternal death (its end). And "life" is, besides natural life, the life of grace and, finally, that eternal life in which grace finds its full flowering, first for the soul and, on the last day, for the body. Certain texts combine these various meanings: e.g., the parallel drawn in the Letter to the Romans between Adam and Christ with regard to original sin.[64] The wages of sin is death, in all the senses of the word, whereas the gift of God is everlasting life in Christ.[65]

There are still other antitheses related to those already considered. To the state of unredeemed nature in which man is under the dominion of sin, we find opposed the justification due to grace merited by Christ. Our Lord's

63. Rom. 8,9-10,16.
64. Rom. 5,12-21.
65. Rom. 6,21,23; 7,10.

redemptive sacrifice replaces the sentence of condemnation, which formerly threatened sinners, with the sentence of justification by which they have been reconciled with God.[66] Christians, formerly slaves to sin, have become slaves to justice; but this slavery is the supreme instance of freedom; it is actually emancipation.[67] They were once darkness, but now they are light and should behave accordingly.[68] The veil which covered their eyes as they tried to read Scripture is henceforth removed and their uncovered faces reflect the glory of the Lord[69] as they prepare to look directly on his countenance in unending happiness.[70] They have passed from the shadows to the reality.[71]

These various antitheses all point to another more fundamental one of which they are partial expressions: the opposition between the two heads of mankind, Adam and Christ. Adam is the figure, the type of him who was to come,[72] and Christ is his antitype. Adam cast his descendants into sin and death; Christ, through his Passion and Resurrection, has brought them life and assured them of salvation. Christ's coming and redemptive death have wrought a deep transformation. Calvary has resulted in a decisive change, a superabundant reparation of the ravages caused by the sin of the first man and aggravated by all the sins of his descendants:

Therefore as from the offense of the one man the result was condemnation to all men, so from the one's fulfillment of a mandate the result is the sanctification which gives life

66. Rom. 5,15-19.
67. Rom. 6,16-19; 1 Cor. 7,21-22.
68. Eph. 5,8; 1 Thess. 5,4-5; Rom. 13,12.
69. 2 Cor. 3,14-18.
70. 1 Cor. 13,12
71. Heb. 10,4.
72. Rom. 5,14.

to all men. In other words, just as by the disobedience of
the one man the many were constituted sinners, so also by
the obedience of the one the many will be constituted holy.
... The greater the offense became, so much the more has
grace increased. So, just as sin has resulted in the reign of
death, so also grace, which confers holiness leading to eternal life, holds sway through Jesus Christ our Lord.[73]

It is always necessary to come back to this central, awe-
inspiring teaching to explain the other Pauline antitheses:
the unfortunate solidarity of men in Adam has been re-
paired by their solidarity in Jesus the Redeemer. And this
second solidarity is much easier to understand than the
former one, for the factors which have intervened—God's
merciful grace, the gifts of justice and life consequent on
Christ's redemptive work—are far more powerful than sin
and the death which flows from it. The Christian is no
longer under the outdated reign of the letter, which kills
by closing the eyes of those who read Scripture and refuse
to recognize Christ; he is under the new reign of the spirit,
which gives life by showing that the old economy prepared
for Christ and led to him.[74] Thus the Apostle can conclude
triumphantly, envisaging both the present effects of the
Redemption and their ultimate fulfillment in the resurrection of the body: "...since man is the cause of death, so
man is the cause of the resurrection from the dead. Just
as in Adam all men die, so too in Christ all men are made
alive."[75]

There can no longer be any question, then, of having
to fulfill the Mosaic observances, of circumcision or uncircumcision. The Mosaic Law was merely a provisional institution; excellent as it was from many viewpoints (despite

73. Rom. 8,18-21.
74. Rom. 7,6; 2 Cor. 3,6.
75. 1 Cor. 15,21-22.

the multiplication of sins it occasioned through the malice of men[76]), the parentheses are henceforth closed. The only circumcision which has weight now is that of the heart, not that of the flesh.[77]

> Being circumcised means nothing; not being circumcised means nothing. It is the keeping of God's commandments that counts. . . . What really counts is not circumcision or its absence, but being a new creature.[78]

Here we have the key to the entire Pauline dialectic: all the oppositions, antitheses, and apparent contradictions are resolved in the renewal wrought by Christ and the obligation of cooperating in it, in a life dominated and constantly inspired by faith and the action of God's Spirit.

Personifications: Sin, Death, Life, and Grace

These exalted teachings are expressed in an unusually vivid and original way which reflects the unique temperament of St. Paul.

The ravages of sin and the blessings of redemption through Christ are for him ever-present and deeply felt realities. Far from conceiving them as abstractions, he personifies them, thus enhancing his rigorous logic with dramatic imagination.

He shows Sin making its entrance into the world, first at the instigation of the devil and then in the wake of Adam's sin.[79] Armed, as it were, from head to foot, it exercises its evil power over all mankind; its kingdom is opposed to the Kingdom of God.[80] It dwells in man and draws him

76. Gal. 3,19.
77. Rom. 2,28-29.
78. 1 Cor. 7,19; Gal. 6,15.
79. 2 Cor. 11,3; Rom. 5,12.
80. Rom. 5,21; 6,12.

toward evil;[81] it holds him in bondage.[82] It perverts the Law and takes advantage of it to enkindle unholy desires,[83] thus exploiting to the utmost its radical opposition to God.[84] Christ alone can annul its power and deliver man from it.[85]

Paradoxically, Sin is abetted in its ravages by the Law given to Israel. Although that Law is spiritual, holy, just, and good,[86] it has nevertheless had the effect of multiplying sins. The Apostle goes so far as to say, in an elliptical expression of his teaching, that it was promulgated to make evil abound,[87] doubtless to make man feel more keenly his misery and need of God's help.[88] "Sin's force comes from the Law,"[89] and, on the other hand, faith in Jesus Christ justifies man and gives him life[90] when it is quickened by love.[91]

Another and more sinister ally of Sin is Death, both bodily and spiritual. It entered the world through and with Sin,[92] and it has reigned with Sin over men.[93] Sin is as it were Death's sting or poisoned dart;[94] Death is the wages legally due to sin;[95] and Sin therefore leads inexorably to Death. For this reason Death is the supreme enemy, the "last enemy" which Christ will destroy.[96] Its defeat will show

---

81. Rom. 7,20.
82. Rom. 6,6,16-20.
83. Rom. 7,8-11.
84. Rom. 7,13.
85. Rom. 8,2-3.
86. Rom. 7,12.
87. Gal. 3,19.
88. Rom. 5,20.
89. 1 Cor. 15,56.
90. Gal. 2,20; 3,11; Rom 1,17; Eph. 2,8.
91. Gal. 5,6.
92. Rom. 5,12.
93. Rom. 5,14-17.
94. 1 Cor. 15,56.
95. Rom. 6,23.
96. 1 Cor. 15,26.

forth the definitive triumph of Christ: he will swallow up Death in that triumph and thus show that the reign of Sin has come to an end.[97]

Confronting Death we see Life, similarly personified: the very life of Christ, who makes himself our life by communicating it to us[98] through Grace. Grace now abounds where Sin had flourished; it reigns through justice for everlasting Life, even as Sin had reigned for Death,[99] and Paul invokes it on behalf of his correspondents at the beginning of each of his Letters.

Many other personifications could be mentioned: Flesh and Spirit, mentioned above, which are always portrayed as adversaries[100] vying for man's allegiance in a deadly contest in which the stakes are eternal life;[101] Circumcision and Uncircumcision;[102] the Kingdom of God, to which the Father calls us[103] and into which he has led us by rescuing us from the powers of darkness;[104] the Cross of Christ, which is at the same time the main object of Paul's teaching,[105] the ensemble of the effects produced by Christ's redemptive sac-

97. 1 Cor. 15,54-57.
98. Col. 3,4.
99. Rom. 5,20-21.
100. Rom. 8,5-8.
101. Rom. 8,12-13.
102. Gal. 6,15; Rom. 3,30.
103. 1 Thess. 2,12.
104. Col. 1,13. Circumcision designates, besides the material rite, the people of Israel and the Mosaic Order as a whole, of which it was one of the main institutions (Gal. 2,7, 12; 5,6; 6,15; Rom. 4,11-12). The Kingdom of God is at times the ensemble of messianic blessings and the everlasting inheritance merited by Christ (1 Thess. 2,12; Col. 1,13; 2 Tim. 4,1), and at times the moral requirements laid down as a condition for entering it (Rom. 14,17; 1 Cor. 6,9; Gal. 5,21; etc.).
105. 1 Cor. 1,17-18; 24-25.

rifice,[106] and that sacrifice itself to which the Apostle unites himself and in which he glories.[107]

The evocative power which the reader of St. Paul finds nearly irresistible stems in part from these personifications, but it also involves other peculiarities of expression which we have yet to point out.

Other Peculiarities of St. Paul's Style

The conciseness of St. Paul's thought, to which we have already called attention, has the effect of making one idea evoke another, often by a mere allusion. When this happens, there is an extreme fullness of doctrine, but the expression of it is so elliptical that we must take into consideration the Apostle's entire doctrinal framework to understand it.

An excellent example of this phenomenon is the solemn introduction to the Letter to the Romans:

> Paul, servant of Jesus Christ to all God's beloved, saints by vocation, at Rome, grace be to you and peace from God our Father and from the Lord Jesus Christ. We have been called to the apostolate and set apart to proclaim the Good News now made known by God, as he had promised it of old through his prophets in Holy Writ. This Good News concerns his Son, who in regard to his human nature was born of the line of David, but who in regard to his all-holy divine nature was constituted the mighty Son of God by his resurrection from the dead, Jesus Christ our Lord. Through him we have received grace and the apostolic office, whose purpose is to bring men of all nations to honor his name by the submission of faith. Among these nations you, who have been called to belong to Jesus Christ, are included.[108]

106. Col. 1,20; Eph. 2,16.
107. Gal. 2,9; 6,14
108. Rom. 1,1-7.

St. Paul's customary greeting is here drawn out in an exceptionally pregnant sentence. Paul identifies himself, as usual, but the title of "apostle" calls to mind the object of his apostolate: the Good News foretold by the prophets and centered around God's Son, Jesus Christ. Now Jesus belongs, by reason of of his human nature, to the line of David; but he is also Son of God, and by his Resurrection he has attained the full exercise of his power as befits his divine nature (literally, his "spirit of holiness"). Once risen, he is forever glorified, even outwardly, as Lord and equal to God. This is the Christ who called Paul to the faith and to the apostolate. This is the Christ who sent Paul to evangelize the pagans in particular, who formed the greater part of the Christian community at Rome. They too have been called by Jesus Christ. Then the Apostle finally gets to his greeting: grace be to you and peace. He has thus given in a few words a full summary of his teaching and the special nature of his mission. His insistence on these points is doubtless motivated by the fact that he is writing to a community which he had not himself evangelized and to which he is confiding his intention to visit.[109] This salutation can be completely understood, however, only if it is correlated to the more fully developed teachings of the other Letters; some commentary is therefore needed in this case.

The doctrine of justification through faith, which St. Paul sets forth after describing his meeting with Peter at Antioch,[110] brings to mind such related matters as Abraham's justification, wrought by faith in the messianic promises and not by the Mosaic Law.[111] The same must be said of the Christological passage in Colossians and the magnificent

109. Rom. 1,8-15.
110. Gal. 2,14-21.
111. Gal. 3,6-14.

prologue to the Ephesian Letter.[112] To spell out in detail the riches of this last passage does not lie in the power of everyone, but it is a rewarding task for those who can do it.

Another point which should be made here is that St. Paul's thought, precisely because of its richness and doubtless also because of his custom of dictating his Letters, does not always immediately achieve its definitive expression. The Apostle sometimes uses a pattern of progressive developments which may seem to a superficial reader to be mere repetitions, but each of which actually adds a new precision or element. This device may be compared to a rising tide which seems to retreat after each wave but actually advances higher with the next one.[113] In the parallel between Adam and Christ,[114] for example, the Apostle first declares pithily that Adam is "a type of him who was to come," thus suggesting that we have a solidarity in Christ just as in Adam. But he does not explicitly affirm this new solidarity until he has shown that it is surer and more efficacious than our solidarity in Adam because God's goodness and the gifts of grace and divine life are more powerful than sin and death. Three concentric circles[115] then oppose the divine life to the reign of death, the sentence of forgiveness for all sins to that of the first man's condemnation, and the reign of the faithful in supernatural life to the reign of death. Only then does Paul at last declare with triumphant assurance: "Just as by the disobedience of the one man the many were constituted sinners, so also by the

112. Col. 15,20; Eph. 1,3-14.
113. A similar procedure is found in St. John, although his approach is somewhat different from that of St. Paul. Cf. Brunot, *op. cit.*, pp. 57-58.

obedience of the one the many will be constituted holy."[116]

The same rhetorical device is found in the ensuing explanation of baptism.[117] The Apostle shows, first of all, that the Christian has died to sin and been born to new life. This transformation has taken place in baptism, which unites the catechumen to Christ's death, burial, and Resurrection; he is therefore inserted into Christ, dying and living with him. His death is a death to the "old man," a death to sin; and his life, a life for God in Christ. The conclusion is that the Christian has been delivered from sin as radically as one can be by death, and that upon this mystical death there follows a sharing in the life of the risen Christ. One might study from a similar viewpoint the moving and difficult passage on reward after death, in the Second Letter to the Corinthians.[118]

Again, St. Paul has a habit of mentioning briefly at the beginning of a Letter a central point to be developed later. In Galatians, for example, the initial affirmation that Christ died for our sins[119] serves as an introduction to the Letter's main point—the powerlessness of the Law to justify. The allusion to the Parousia at the beginning of the Thessalonian Letters serves the same function in relation to their essential content.[120]

In other instances, unequally developed arguments dovetail to produce an apodictic conclusion; yet the premises and the relative value of each argument come to light only on reflection. This is the case with the Apostle's judgment regarding women,[121] and still more where he shows

116. V. 19.
117. Rom. 6,1-11.
118. 2 Cor. 5,1-10.
119. Gal. 1,4.
120. 1 Thess. 1,10; 2 Thess. 1,6-10.
121. 1 Cor. 1,2-16.

the impotence of the Law.[122] Very often St. Paul combines, with no concern for order, his personal opinions and advice, on the one hand, with the most lofty theological specula- tions, on the other; 2 Corinthians and Galatians are typical in this respect. But it also happens at times that the ar- gumentation is developed in a magnificent crescendo as in Romans,[123] where Paul shows that our total glorification through bodily resurrection is longed for by inanimate crea- tures, ardently desired not only by ourselves but by the Holy Spirit, and ultimately willed by the Father. Then the Apostle bursts into a triumphant tone and extols the rock- like character of Christian hope: "If God is for us, who is against us?"[124]

This last passage, overflowing with lyricism, makes us think of a hymn. Nor is it the only one of its kind. It is commonly agreed that the important Christological pas- sage of Philippians[125] is a hymn edited or even composed (not too unlikely a hypothesis) by St. Paul. Again, the same literary characteristics can be found in the majestic intro- duction to the Ephesian Letter, as well as later on in the same Letter:[126]

> There is one body and one Spirit, even as you, from the moment you were called, had the one hope your calling imparted. There is one Lord, one Faith, one Baptism, one God and Father of all, who rules all things and pervades all things and sustains all things.

It is easy to discern a similar rhythm and doctrinal richness in this passage from the First Letter to Timothy:

> And by common acknowledgment great is the mystery of

122. Gal. 2,15-21.
123. Rom. 8,19-30.
124. Rom. 8,31
125. Phil. 2,5-11.
126. Eph. 1,3-14; 4,4-5.

the true religion: He was made visible in his human nature, vindicated in his spiritual nature, seen by angels, preached among the Gentiles, accorded faith in the world, taken up in glory.[127]

The "A,B,A' " Developments

St. Paul's literary temperament and the eloquence of his style are also evident in another peculiarity on which recent exegesis has rightly placed great emphasis. Found in at least seven of his Letters, this device consists in the following arrangement of ideas. First he states a proposition (A); then he adds some considerations which seem more or less to be digressions (B). And finally, he returns to the main thought (A') re-inforced and justified, now, by the apparent parenthesis. There are many examples of this A,B,A' structure, in the Letters of the Captivity as well as in the earlier ones; and this is an important point in establishing the authenticity of the whole Pauline corpus. An almost complete listing of these instances can be found in Brunot;[128] it will suffice, for present purposes, to point out a few examples.

The procedure is especially common, first of all, in the Letter to the Romans. To the revelation of God's justice (A)[129] is opposed the revelation of his wrath, earned by all sinful men, pagans and Jews alike (B).[130] Then Paul returns again to the manifestation of God's justice won through the blood of Christ (A').[131] In this case the long digression on sin's universal sway shows the need for justification to escape God's punishment. Later on, in the fifth through

127. 1 Tim. 3,16.
128. F. Brunot, *op cit.*, pp. 42-48.
129. Rom. 1,17.
130. Rom. 1,18-3,20.
131. Rom. 3,21-30.

the eighth chapter, Paul uses the same three-stage device to show that God's love is the source of our salvation. Theme A is expressed in 5:1-11; the Apostle then shows that Christ has removed the three obstacles to that love: Sin, Death, and the Mosaic Law—this is B.[132] Only after that explanation can he conclude, on a triumphant note, to the efficacy of God's love, manifested through the gift and action of the Holy Spirit (A').[133]

The identical structure can be seen once again in the following section of the same Letter: viz., the ninth to eleventh chapter, which deal with Israel's unbelief. A: Israel as a whole did not believe in Christ, and this rejection shows God's sovereign liberty in distributing his gifts;[134] B: this rejection is explained by Israel's attitude in refusing to accept the message of salvation, failing to grasp its gratuitous and universal character;[135] A': God has nevertheless rejected his own people only partially and temporarily: one day Israel will embrace the gospel.[136]

The same procedure proliferates in the two Corinthian Letters and is no less striking in the Letters of the Captivity. At the beginning of Colossians,[137] St. Paul sets forth Christ's transcendance and primacy (A); he then declares that the revelation of this mystery has been entrusted to him;[138] and he concludes by showing his correspondents how the faithful share in this mystery—by a fullness of understanding and by an intimate union achieved through love (A').[139]

132. Rom. 5,12-7,25.
133. Rom. 8,1-38.
134. Rom. 9,6-29.
135. Rom. 9,30-10,21.
136. Rom. 11,1-36
137. Col. 1,15-23.
138. Col. 1,24-29.
139. Col. 2,1-3.

The whole first part of Ephesians is built on a similar rhythm, as, for instance, in the passage where Paul shows that the risen Christ is the supreme leader and head of the Church, his body (A),[140] then declares in eloquent language that the incorporation of the faithful into Christ was effected by the Redemption, a wholly gratuitous work due to the Father's loving initiative (B).[141] Finally he affirms that by the Redemption, which knows no favoritism, the pagans have been reconciled to Israel and all men thenceforth incorporated into one "new man" in Jesus Christ (A').[142] And this is the capital truth at the very heart of the Pauline gospel.

This teaching was the Good News brought to the world by our Savior, who died not only "to save the whole nation, but to unite in one body all the scattered children of God";[143] and Paul is its humble and enthusiastic herald par excellence.[144] It is hardly surprising that truths which are at first sight so disconcerting (and which the Judeo-Christians found it so hard to accept) should at times receive from his pen the paradoxical expression which has been pointed out above.

These expressions are no longer difficult to understand, however, once the reader has become familiar with the Apostle's style; and they have the same disarming, irresistible effect on his readers as they did on his listeners. We are quite willing to overlook Paul's outbursts and abruptness, once we have come to know the fiery temperament which accounts for them—that burning ardor constantly overflowing with love for Christ and men. And we can

140. Eph. 1,20-23.
141. Eph. 2,1-10.
142. Eph. 2,11-22.
143. Jn. 11,52.
144. Eph. 3,1-12.

likewise excuse certain subtleties which reflect his rabbinical background, like the Sara-Agar allegory[145] or even the strange observation that the descendant promised to Abraham had to be Christ, in the final analysis, because the word "descendant" is a singular, not a plural term.[146] Having come to appreciate St. Paul's style, we can easily see that these are secondary considerations brought up in passing, to which he does not attribute the same conclusiveness as he does to the more basic arguments by which he shows that the Law of Moses has been rescinded and redemption won for us through the blood of Christ.

145. Gal. 4,21-31.
146. Gal. 3,16.

Chapter Three

ST. PAUL'S DOCTRINE

The Doctrinal Significance of the Vision on the Way to Damascus

The doctrinal richness of St. Paul's Letters is already apparent from the preceding chapters; volumes have been written to synthesize and explain the teachings they contain. Our aim in this chapter is necessarily a more modest one: it is to examine briefly a few salient aspects of St. Paul's teaching for which some prior introduction is particularly necessary.[1]

Christ's sudden appearance on the way to Damascus not only left a permanent impression on Paul's character; it made a totally new man of him. Saul the persecutor was cast to the ground, and a different man arose: Paul, the Christian and Apostle. Enlightened to the very depths of his soul despite the temporary physical blindness caused to the heavenly vision,[2] he hastened to be baptized by Ananias and without delay "began to preach Jesus as the Son of God" to his stunned countrymen.[3] The sight of Jesus of Nazareth, risen and glorified, convinced Paul of the authenticity of Christ's mission, the efficacy of his sacrifice, and his divinity. In the years that followed, enlightened

---

1. Fuller expositions of St. Paul's doctrinal theology are listed in the bibliography.
2. Ac. 26,19.
3. Ac. 8,17-22.

by the Holy Spirit and instructed both by the other Apostles and by his own missionary experiences, the Vessel of Election was gradually to draw out the implications of this central truth.

Of the many such implications developed in Paul's Letters, three are particularly fundamental: the Resurrection of Jesus Christ, the abolition of the Mosaic Law and justification through Jesus Christ, and the intimate union between all the faithful and Christ as well as among themselves. This last truth was communicated to Paul in an especially vivid way when he learned, on the way to Damascus, that to persecute the Christians was to persecute Jesus himself.

Paul was to preach the Passion tirelessly, to the point where he could claim to have "portrayed" Jesus Christ crucified before the eyes of his hearers.[4] But he never separated the Resurrection from the redemptive sacrifice of which it formed the crown and fulfillment. He probably had never known Christ during his mortal life,[5] but he had seen Jesus risen, and this vision had made him a true Apostle.[6] He was always to retain in his heart his unforgettable confrontation with "the Lord to whom belongs all glory.[7] He constantly refers to the Resurrection as the decisive event without which the Christian faith would be vain and without object.[8] He is filled with wonder when he contemplates the sovereign power exercised by our heavenly Father in raising and glorifying his Son.[9] He sees Christ's Resurrection as the model and the cause (through the merits of the

4. Gal. 3,1.
5. 2 Cor. 5,16.
6. 1 Cor. 9,1; 15,8.
7. 1 Cor. 2,8.
8. 1 Cor. 15, 14,17.
9. Eph. 1,20-22.

Cross) of the Christian's spiritual rebirth, and as the pledge of that bodily resurrection which will on the last day crown the entire redemptive work.[10] Thus he could sum up his whole kerygma, in writing to the faithful at Rome, in this short formula: "If you confess with your lips that Jesus is the Lord, and believe in your heart that God raised him from the dead, you shall be saved."[11]

Justification through Faith

It is a known fact that the Letters to the Galatians and the Romans are filled with the doctrine of justification through faith in Jesus Christ, to the exclusion of the works of the Mosaic Law. But this doctrine should be well understood and all ambiguity avoided in connection with it.

St. Paul never speaks of faith as a purely intellectual process through which the mind adheres to the gospel message. He conceives the Christian's faith *existentially*, in the image of his own—as *both* a confession of Christ's divinity *and* a total and irrevocable gift of his person to Him in whom he recognized the Son of God, the Lord equal to Yahweh.[12] "What shall I do, Lord"[13] —Paul has thrust his whole being into this reply to the risen Christ. A theoretical law devoid of influence on life is inconceivable for him. The faith that justifies is "faith that expresses itself in love," faith accompanied by "good deeds which God prepared beforehand for us to practice."[14]

Besides trust in Christ's word, faith involves sorrow for

10. Rom. 6,4-11; Phil. 3,10-11; 1 Cor. 15,20-22. St. Thomas Aquinas was later to add that Christ's Resurrection is also the very *instrument* through which God will accomplish our own.
11. Rom. 10,9.
12. Phil. 2,11.
13. Ac. 22,10.
14. Gal. 5,6; Eph. 2,10.

past sins and the resolve to conform one's life to God's commandments. The Apostle insists over and over on the avoidance of sin, the putting to death of the "old man" who must give way to the "new man,"[15] the assiduous practice of all the virtures crowned and unified by love.[16] This resolute commitment, this existential act of faith with all it involves, culminates in a request for baptism and a radical transformation which makes the Christian a "new creation."[17] The dynamic power of this expression makes it clear that "justification through faith in Christ"[18] is a truncated expression in which *only one element* of conversion to Christianity stands for the whole ensemble of dispositions and steps involved in such a conversion. Unless this cardinal point is constantly borne in mind when reading St. Paul's Letters, there is an ever-present danger of seriously misunderstanding the Apostle's thought.

Justification through faith in Christ presupposes by contrast that "the deeds the Law prescribes" are powerless to obtain justification.[19] If the deeds of the Law could justify, observes the Apostle, we would have to conclude that Christ died "to no purpose"[20] and that the sacrifice of Calvary was useless, which is obviously absurd. The Law was nailed to the cross by Christ;[21] it is henceforth abolished and cannot be imposed on converts. We know that this was a point of contention in the primitive Church. Christians of Jewish origin, deeply and religiously devoted to the Law, found it very difficult to admit that it had been rescinded and no

15. Rom. 6,6; Eph. 2,22-24.
16. 1 Cor. 13; Col. 3,14.
17. Gal. 6,15.
18. Gal. 2,16; Rom. 1,17.
19. Gal. 2,16.
20. Gal. 2,21.
21. Col. 2,14.

longer obliged. Peter himself had to be enlightened on this point by a special vision before he would let Cornelius and his family be baptized.[22] And he had to give an accounting of himself to the Christians of Jerusalem who had not yet overcome their own prejudices in the matter and gave in only with great reluctance.[23]

The matter came to a climax soon afterwards at Antioch, when emissaries from Jerusalem confronted Peter with some serious difficulties. St. Peter temporized with their demands, and St. Paul "resisted him to his face" to vindicate the rights of Christian liberty with regard to the Jewish Law.[24] As the Apostle to the Gentiles well knew, the pagans would never have embraced the gospel if they first had to become Jews and submit to circumcision and the other Mosaic observances. The matter was soon taken up by the Apostles and elders at the famous Council of Jerusalem, and the testimony given by Paul, Barnabas, Peter, and James resulted in a triumph for freedom. Nothing should be imposed on converts from paganism, the Council decreed, except some dietary regulations which would facilitate common meals and the common celebration of the Eucharist.[25]

Immediately following the incident at Antioch, Paul had already sent to the Galatian churches a somewhat theoretical and sketchy demonstration of the Law's powerlessness to justify.[26] Now, writing to the Romans, he decided to treat

22. Ac. 10.
23. Ac. 11,1-18.
24. Gal. 2,11,4. The incident is related with appealing emotion in Gal. 2,11-21. The disagreement between the two Apostles had to do not with doctrine, but only with the practical attitude to be adopted with regard to converts from paganism.
25. Ac. 15,1-32.
26. Gal. 3,1-5,2.

the same subject more calmly and thoroughly.[27] His line of reasoning in these chapters deserves careful consideration. First he shows with keen precision and skill that Abraham, the great forefather from whom all Israel rightly claimed to be descended, was justified by his faith in God's promise of a numberless posterity, and not by the Mosaic Law which was promulgated several centuries later.[28] Nor, as a matter of fact, was Abraham justified by circumcision; for him the rite was not a condition for justification, but the outward sign of the justice and holiness already obtained by his faith.[29] The Christian is in his turn justified by faith in Jesus Christ, which has basically the same object as the faith of Abraham, namely the divine promises, no longer to be fulfilled in the future but already superabundantly fulfilled in Jesus Christ.[30] It is always by faith, then, that God justifies, both before the promulgation of the Mosaic Law and after its abolition. When the Law was in force, from the time of Moses until Christ's Resurrection, it was a factor in the justification of Old Testament saints only because there was joined to it the need for faith in the divine promise, just as in Abraham's case. The deeds of the Law never could justify of themselves. If they could, the whole gratuitous and transcendent character of the supernatural order, which the Apostle rightly stresses, would be compromised. Man is not justified by his works; faith itself is a gift of God. In no way can man glory in being the author of his own salvation.[31]

St. Paul's global and somewhat simplified presentation of this important subject takes into consideration two dis-

27. Rom. 1-8.
28. Gal. 3,6-9, 16-18.
29. Rom. 4,1-12.
30. Rom. 4,16-25.
31. Gal. 5,5-6; 1 Cor. 1,28-31; Rom. 3,27-28; Eph. 2,8-10.

tinct groups of people, without distinguishing too clearly between them. On the one hand there were the *converts* from Judaism who thought the Law was still in force; and on the other, the all-too-numerous *Jews themselves*, who pretended, in their pride, to observe the Law and the traditions added to it by the purely human authority of the rabbis. This latter group, in particular, completely failed to see the need of calling on God for help; they therefore ended up in an impasse, in an attitude both pharisaical and pelagian before the letter. The Law simply did not justify without that faith which alone could obtain the divine help necessary to observe it.[32]

There is a final point which should be made in this connection. When the Apostle uses the word "law," he usually means the Mosaic Law. But he also uses this term in a more general sense, as when he speaks of the natural law written in the heart of every man[33] or when he observes that by laying down a precept, every positive law runs the risk of exciting in sinful man the desire for the fruit it forbids.[34] Here again, therefore, the reader must pay close attention to the context in which the term is used.

The Parousia

The problem of the Mosaic observances was, to be sure, one of St. Paul's crosses. But it also had its good effect on his teaching: it led him to stress, not only the universality of God's call to faith which transcended national barriers,[35] but also the unity of God's plan and the continuity of the two Covenants.

Another source of difficulty for the Apostle was the prob-

32. Cf. Prat, *op. cit.*, vol. 1, pp. 168-204.
33. Rom. 2,12-16.
34. Rom. 7,7-23.
35. Eph. 2,11-22; Rom. 4,11.

lem of Christ's return, or the "Parousia." This is a delicate
question, fraught with obscurities, but we have Paul to
thank for at least partially dispelling these difficulties and
thus lifting to some extent the veil which still hides from us
the consummation of the universe. The term "parousia,"
which means "presence," was often used to designate
the visit of an important person. In the New Testament,
and particularly in St. Paul, it also denotes Christ's glorious
return at the end of time, so ardently longed for by primitive Christianity.[36] St. Paul himself shared this longing, and
the same must have been true of every Christian, for the
Parousia will mark the consummation of the Redemption;
it will herald that total and definitive establishment of
God's Kingdom which we pray for daily in the Our Father
without, perhaps, fully realizing the implications of our
prayer.[37]

Now, an ill-informed concept of this hope had occasioned, particularly in Thessalonica, the conviction that the
Savior's return was imminent—even to the point where
some of the faithful were living in scandalous idleness.[38]
It is true that because of his style Paul sometimes seems
to include himself among those who will still be living at
the moment of the Parousia, but we have already pointed
out that this is a figure of speech.[39] Elsewhere in the same
Thessalonian Letters he seems to say that he will die first
and rise again when Christ returns.[40] He does the same thing
whenever he approaches this subject,[41] and we can justly

36. 1 Thess. 2,19; 3,13, etc.; 2 Thess. 2,1; 8,9; 1 Cor. 15,23.
37. Cf. 1 Cor. 15,23-28.
38. This idleness is roundly condemned by the Apostle in 1
    Thess. 4,11-2 and, especially, 2 Thess. 3,6-15.
39. 1 Thess. 4,15-17; 1 Cor. 15,51-52; cf. above, p. 24.
40. 1 Thess. 5,5-10. 1 Cor. 6,14.
41. Cf. 2 Cor. 5,1-4; 6-10; Rom. 13,11-12; 14,7-8; Phil. 3,20;
    4,5; 1,21-23; 3,11; 2 Tim. 4,1,6-8.

conclude from this that he had no real idea when the cataclysmic event would actually take place.[42] As far as Paul is concerned, an early date and a remote one are equally possible for our Lord's return, and this explains why he places himself first in one and then in the other perspective. Doubtless he did hope for an imminent Parousia, but to hope for or desire something is not to affirm it. He cannot logically be charged with error on this point, any more than we can be called wrong when, considering the slow progress made by the gospel, we tend to think of the Parousia as centuries away from us. In reality, of course, we know no more about its date than Paul did, and like him we too can affirm nothing certain in the matter.

Another point which helps clarify St. Paul's teaching in this matter is that according to the Apostle himself, the conversion of the pagans, and then that of the Jews, will precede the Parousia.[43] This suggests a somewhat prolonged delay. Besides, he also dwells on the formidable struggles and apostasies which will precede Christ's return,[44] although he does so in terms whose obscurity is common to all the apocalyptic passages of the New Testament. Nevertheless, he does clearly teach two points worth bearing in mind. The first is that death brings into union with Christ those whose lives have been conformed to the gospel (from which we rightly conclude to a particular judgment which precedes the general judgment).[45] And the second is that the last generation of human beings, which will witness the

---

42. In this Paul was a faithful echo of our Lord himself who left the time of his return shrouded in impenetrable mystery. Jesus even went so far as to deny that he knew the date of the Parousia, probably meaning that it was not yet possible for him to reveal it; see Mt. 24,36.
43. Rom. 9-11.
44. 2 Thess. 2,1-12.
45. 2 Cor. 5,6-10; Phil. 1,20-26.

Parousia, will have the privilege of not passing through death;[46] their bodies will be transformed "in the twinkling of an eye" and made like the bodies of the dead already risen.

Obviously this perspective was able to enkindle immoderate desires; death is repugnant to all, and Paul himself would have liked to escape it, but without, let us repeat it, having any certitude of doing so.[47] This wish was, however, vain; toward the end of his life he contemplated his impending martyrdom calmly and fearlessly, his spirit completely absorbed in the thought of his eternal reward.[48] Even here, however, his vision includes the Parousia—the manifestation of Christ prepared for and in a way anticipated by the glorification of his servants. There is a definite continuity and conpenetration between the earthly phase and the heavenly fulfillment of the redemptive mystery, just as the life of the justified Christian is of the same nature as eternal life.[49] The gift of the Holy Spirit, the pledge of our heavenly inheritance,[50] constitutes a real, though inchoate and incomplete, possession of what will be given us in eternity.[51]

46. 1 Thess. 4,15-18; 1 Cor. 15,51-53.
47. 2 Cor. 5,2-4.
48. 2 Tim. 4,6-8.
49. Grace and glory differ only in this, that the life of grace is characterized by obscurity and that of glory by vision of God face to face (1 Cor. 13,12).
50. 2 Cor. 1,22; 5,5; Eph. 1,14.
51. This subject deserves fuller development than is possible here; see the author's *Key Concepts of St. Paul* (see bibliography), pp. 259-85, and Prat, *op. cit.*, pp. 352-82. The only point to be stressed here is that St. Paul is guilty of no error with regard to the Parousia.

The Continuity of the Two Covenants;
St. Paul's Use of Scripture

This unity of God's redemptive plan is, in fact, another central point of St. Paul's teaching. Two aspects of it are particularly evident in his Letters: first, the unity and continuity of the two Covenants; and second, the basic identity between the state of the justified Christian here below and the glorified state promised him hereafter.

The prophetic character of the Old Testament and its fulfillment in the New is one of the points on which the Apostle was profoundly enlightened by the divine Spirit.[52] Christ is for him the "YES" par excellence, in whom all God's promises to Israel find their fulfilment.[53] He explicitly cites the Old Testament over two hundred times, and a rapid glance through an annotated translation of his Letters makes it easy to verify that besides these explicit citations there are continual allusions made in conformity with the rabbinic custom of using biblical texts to support their assertions. The citations are most often made according to the Greek Septuagint text in which ancient Christians read the Old Testament, since most of the converts did not know Hebrew.[54] At times they are only approximate, made from memory, or used as simple illustrations of a point by an allusion to Scripture. Thus the rapid spread of the gospel is stressed in Romans with a verse of Psalm 18, which actually deals with the silent language of the stars, heard everywhere.[55] We are obviously not to look upon this sort of accommodation as a true scriptural argument; it is merely

52. Rom. 1,2; 3,21.
53. 2 Cor. 1,19-20.
54. This is the case, e.g., with Paul's citation of Deut. 30,11-14 in Rom. 10,6-9.
55. Rom. 10,18.

a literary device accepted and used freely by Jews of the time. But Paul also makes use of true prophecies: e.g., when he declares that Christ died for our sins and rose again "according to the Scriptures."[56] He often cites the Bible in its literal sense, as is the case with his references to Osee in the Letter to the Romans.[57] These and other like instances present no difficulty.

At other times the Apostle gives to the text he cites a fullness of meaning that the sacred author most likely did not glimpse but which was willed by the Spirit of God and which Paul now sees in the full light of the gospel revelation. Thus justification by the Law in Heb. 2:4 signified directly that faith in the divine promises would be rewarded by the ending of the Babylonian Captivity, but the Apostle sees in this earthly liberation a prophecy of true deliverance, of messianic salvation which will consist in liberation from sin and will be the source of true life. The prophet's oracle, "The just man, because of his faith, shall live," is thus deepened in a direction which does no violence to it because in both cases there is involved an absolute trust in God's word.[58] Divine revelation regarding the nature of this faith or trust was still incomplete at the time the prophet lived, but it was completed by Christ.[59] St. Paul then bolsters his argument with a citation from the Psalm which declares that no living man is just before God.[60] He applies this in an unrestricted way to the Jews who expected justification from the Law, and he obviously intends this application of Scripture to be taken literally, for he goes on to assert that no one is justified by the deeds of the Law

56. 1 Cor. 15,3-4.
57. Osee 2,24; 1,10, in Rom. 9,25-26.
58. Gal. 3,11; Rom. 1,17.
59. Cf. Heb. 1,2.
60. Ps. 142,2; Gal. 2,16.

and proves this point with other arguments in the verses that follow.[61]

This method of reasoning is based on a more general truth: that the events of the Old Testament are types or prophetic figures of those in the New. Jesus himself made this abundantly clear when he applied to himself the Old Testament texts on the brazen serpent,[62] the manna,[63] the living water,[64] the good shepherd,[65] and the suffering servant;[66] as well as when he called himself the true Bridegroom,[67] the true Vine,[68] the cornerstone,[69] etc. But whereas the Gospels, St. Peter,[70] and the Apocalypse merely *presuppose* this general truth when they show the fulfillment of various prophecies in Christ, St. Paul goes further. He explicitly formulates a general principle on the subject when he declares that the Law was a shadow of "the realities which were to come,"[71] and he applies that principle many times. Adam, for instance, is the type or figure of Christ;[72] Abraham's justification through faith prefigured that of Christians;[73] Christ is the true paschal lamb;[74] the Old Covenant foreshadowed the New, sealed with the blood of Christ;[75] the manna in the desert and the water which flowed

61. Gal. 2,17-21.
62. Jn. 3,14.
63. Jn. 6,32,33,58.
64. Jn. 7,37-38.
65. Jn. 10,11-17.
66. Mt. 27,46.
67. Mk. 2,19-20; Mt. 22,1-14; Mk. 12,1-9.
68. Jn. 15,1-8.
69. Mk. 12,10-11.
70. 1 Pet. 2,22-25.
71. Col. 2,17.
72. Rom. 5,12-19.
73. Rom. 4,17, 23.
74. 1 Cor. 5,7.
75. 1 Cor. 11,25.

from the rock symbolized Christian sacraments.[76] The punishment of the Israelites who could not enter the Promised Land because of their indocility should make Christians fear the divine wrath if they follow that deplorable example;[77] the union of man and woman in marriage should be modeled on that of Christ and the Church.[78] Ancient Israel, the carnal offspring of Adam, prefigured the new Israel according to the spirit, the true Israel of God,[79] which is no longer confined to one nation but embraces the whole of mankind.[80]

St. Paul thus sheds a flood of light on the deeper meaning of the Old Testament and on the unity of God's plan as manifested in Scripture. The veil which covered the face and the heart of Israel in reading the Old Testament will fall once and for all when it is converted to the Lord;[81] the Apostle himself is a striking example of this truth. This way of thinking is unquestionably valid for anyone who admits the inspired and prophetic character of the Bible, but it also furnishes an impressive confirmation of the other types of theological proof.

St. Paul does, by way of exception, use the allegory of Sara and Agar[82] with a subtlety and excessive allegorization traceable to rabbinic methodology, but it is legitimate to ask whether he intends, in so doing, to bring to bear a true demonstration of the rejection of those Israelites who were unfaithful to Christ, or whether he does not merely make use of a certain oratorical accommodation.

76. 1 Cor. 10,1-6.
77. 1 Cor. 10,6-11.
78. Eph. 5,22-23.
79. Gal. 3,7-9, 26; 6,16.
80. Gal. 3,26-28; Col. 3,11.
81. 2 Cor. 3,13-16.
82. Gal. 4,21-31.

From these observations we can conclude that there is a wide variation in the Apostle's use of Scripture; each citation must be carefully weighed in its context to avoid over-extending or minimizing its teaching. Certainly the biblical atmosphere which permeates the Pauline Letters and which St. Paul himself had breathed from his earliest childhood, helped to give him a religious depth and awareness of God's power and mercy, of God's redemptive design and moral demands, but above all, of God's love which was the spiritual patrimony of Israel and conferred on the Chosen People an immortal grandeur despite the deformations inflicted on the message of Moses and the prophets by the casuistry of the Pharisees.

The Continuity between the Life of Grace and Eternal Life

The continuity between the two Covenants is complemented and crowned by the continuity between the life of grace here below and eternal life.

The royal gift of the Holy Spirit makes the Christian a child of his heavenly Father and a brother and co-heir of the Son.[83] The believer is transformed to the depths of his being and placed in a totally new state, which he can no doubt lose by sin, but which differs from eternal life only in degree, not in nature. The Pauline Letters dwell often, from different viewpoints, on this aspect of the redemptive mystery. The Christian is at once in time and in eternity: the obscure parousia, or veiled presence of Christ in his heart[84] is the beginning of the final Parousia in glory; our life, hidden now in God with Christ, will flower with him in glory at his solemn return,[85] and the mystery of the Eu-

83. Gal. 4,6-7; Rom. 8,16-17, 29.
84. Eph. 3,17.
85. Col. 3,3-4.

charist is the bond par excellence between these two comings.[86] The pledge and first-fruits of the Spirit which we now possess[87] herald and guarantee the total gift. We live the life of Christ;[88] the Kingdom of God has begun, even as we await its completion and fulfillment;[89] God calls us to the Kingdom of his glory[90] and has even now led us into it, having rescued us from the powers of darkness.[91] It is in hope that we have been saved,[92] but our salvation is nonetheless partially achieved; we are on the way[93] and in the day of salvation.[94] The great liberation from sin and death has already begun for us; it is up to us to remain constant; we are not destined "to incur wrath, but to gain salvation through our Lord Jesus Christ.[95] We are saved by the grace and goodness of God, through faith;[96] time and eternity merge, and we are citizens of heaven.[97]

We thus see, though all too briefly, how the Apostle explores every facet of this idea. And he is justified in doing so, because the idea is an important one which stresses, for the man of God, the indefectible character of Christian hope, which cannot disappoint[98] and can be frustrated or defeated only by man's deliberate infidelity. This close connection between the temporal and eternal perspectives which continually intermingle in St. Paul's Letters may at

86. 1 Cor. 11,26.
87. 2 Cor. 1,22; 5,5; Eph. 1,14; Rom. 8,23.
88. Gal. 2,20.
89. 1 Cor. 15,24-28.
90. 1 Thess. 2,12.
91. Col. 1,13.
92. Rom. 8,24.
93. Ac. 16,17.
94. 2 Cor. 6,2.
95. 1 Thess. 5,9.
96. Eph. 2,8.
97. Phil. 3,30.
98. Rom. 5,5.

first sight seem obscure, but it is in reality one more aspect of the Apostle's richness of thought; it is one more expression of his magnificent view of God's redemptive plan.

Overall View of the Redemptive Plan

Excessive preoccupation with particular aspects of Paul's thought, through which we have tried to mark out some guidepaths, must not lead the reader to overlook the general structure of the redemptive plan as set forth by the Apostle.

Indeed, the doctrine of the Redemption and the salvation brought to men by Christ shines forth on every page of his Letters. Its main affirmations are easy enough to grasp, especially in the Letter to the Romans; but often St. Paul refers only to one or the other aspect of the matter. He was far less concerned, after all, with giving a systematic exposition than with discharging his duty as an Apostle and providing for the needs of the various Christian communities,[99] where there were delicate conscience cases to solve and false teachers whose strange speculations were to gain in strength during the ensuing centuries and form a source of grave trouble for the Church. The nascent heresies did, nevertheless, have one good effect: they led the Apostle to make his teaching more explicit and to formulate it in a more precise and complete way than he might otherwise have done.

Bearing these points in mind, we can now proceed to furnish a brief presentation of Paul's "gospel":[100] the mystery of universal redemption, the mystery of Jesus Christ who incorporates into his own death and resurrection those who believe in him.

The general prevalence of sin deeply grieved the Apostle.

99. Cf. above, pp. 24-25.
100. Gal. 1,11; Rom. 2,16.

The spectacle of Athens filled with idols had aroused his anger.[101] His Letter to the Christians at Rome contains a graphic description of both pagan corruption and Jewish faithlessness, which places the proud Jew in just as desperate a situation as the sinful pagan.[102] The reign of sin and death is traced back to the disobedience of Adam, who lost God's friendship for all men, unleashed concupiscence and evil passions in their hearts, and left them hopelessly buried in revolt against God. The pagan world did not know how to recognize God in his works; Israel, though favored with divine revelation, united to God by the Covenant of Sinai, guided and enlightened by the Law, had too often shown itself stiff-necked and had failed to observe the divine precepts.

But God was merciful; through his prophets he promised a Messia descended from Abraham, who would repair the ravages wrought by sin and set up a New Covenant, no longer with only one people, but with the whole of mankind. When the fullness of time had come, God sent his only Son, pre-existing, eternal Creator like himself. Born of a woman and of David's line according to the flesh, the Son of God assumed a human nature subject to suffering and death. In his immeasurable love he became obedient even to death on a cross, and was thus constituted, through the eternal will of his Father, the channel of forgiveness for men. His unfathomable obedience brought superabundant reparation for the disobedience of Adam and his descendants. Through faith in him sinners are justified; our blessed solidarity in Jesus Christ more than restores our collective loss in Adam. To proclaim the efficacy of Christ's sacrifice, God has uniquely exalted him by his Resurrection

101. Ac. 17,16.
102. Rom. 1,18-3,20.

and Ascension. Now glorified at the right hand of the Father, Jesus must be adored by all as sovereign Lord equal to Yahweh and as the Redeemer who has reconciled men to God. Such is the Good News brought to men by the Apostles, including Paul himself—eye-witnesses of Christ's exaltation "whose testimony is true" and therefore worthy of belief.[103]

Sinful man is therefore redeemed, now, and dearly bought at the price of Christ's own blood.[104] But God, who has redeemed us with no help from us, will not save us without asking our free collaboration; that is eminently worthy of both God and man. Our reply to the divine call is faith, acceptance by the mind of the Christian message and at the same time a total consecration of the believer's entire being to his Savior. The act of faith itself is a gift of God, which is impossible without grace but is refused to no man of good will. The generous and gratuitous character of the Redemption is thus in every way apparent.

Adherence to Christ leads the convert to ask for baptism, from which there results for him a new birth, forgiveness of sin, and the gift of supernatural life.[105] This bath of regeneration[106] makes man die, be buried, and spiritually rise with Christ: he dies to sin and henceforth lives for God in Christ. To avoid losing his state of justice, the Christian must struggle against concupiscence and the evil tendencies which persist in him. Yet his victory in this difficult spiritual combat is assured; he is more than sufficiently armed by the gift of the Holy Spirit, who strengthens him to crucify his flesh, to live in the practice of love and all the other Christian virtues, and to reproduce in himself the

103. Jn. 19,35.
104. 1 Cor. 6,20; 7,23.
105. Rom. 6,3-11.
106. Tit. 3,5.

image of Christ, reflecting on his face the glory of the Lord so as to be "transformed into his very image from one degree of splendor to another, such as comes from the Lord who is the spirit.[107] The Spirit enlightens and inspires him, gives him all the help he needs to live as a true child of his heavenly Father, as brother of Christ and worthy member of his body, as a temple of the same Spirit. The Eucharist, which commemorates the sacrifice of the Cross and prolongs the offering of that redemptive sacrifice, is the privileged means by which the divine life is shared and increased. This life is dispensed through the Church, whose infallible authority proclaims the teaching of Christ and the Apostles, and whose salutary discipline ensures our fidelity to the requirements of the Christian life.

As a member of that great body of which Christ is the head,[108] the Christian is never alone. He is sustained by the prayer, the example, and the sacrifices of his brothers; he himself knows that his every action must help to build up the body of Christ but can also bring harm to it. Whatever state God has called him to, virginity or marriage, he is constantly aware that he is responsible for his brothers, supernaturally joined to him by a bond whose strength is constantly increased by the Eucharist, the Sacrament of unity.[109] Working for the salvation of all even as he strives for his own, he walks with courage and love toward the glorious life promised to him: "But now, set free from sin and become slaves of God, you have your reward in sanctification, which finally leads to life everlasting."[110]

All men are called to realize this ideal. There is no longer Jew, nor pagan, nor slave, nor free man. And if

107. 2 Cor. 3,18.
108. Col. 3,24; Eph. 1,22-23.
109. 1 Cor. 10,17.
110. Rom. 6,22.

Israel as a whole still wears a blindfold, the day will come when it will recognize in Jesus of Nazareth the Messia foretold by the prophets. Its incredulity led the Apostle to turn to the pagans; but the divine promises cannot be thwarted; the chosen people remains ever beloved of God and will be saved in its turn.

Such is the magnificent work to which the Apostles were consecrated. They brought to it an unflagging courage, a hope that no deception could sway, a supernatural joy impervious to its surroundings of persecution and tribulations of every kind. A terrible drama has been going on, in fact, ever since the fall of the first man at the instigation of the infernal serpent. Christ has conquered that serpent on the Cross and with him sin and death. But the enemies have not lost all their virulence, and so the struggle continues. The mystery of iniquity, the man of sin who would play God, is always with us; apostasies sadden and will continue to sadden the Church. All Christians are actors in this drama and must stand firm to the end. Those who remain faithful will be with Christ forever when death comes to put an end to their labors. And the combat will continue until that day, known to God alone, when the Savior will come down from heaven, destroy the evil one "with the breath of his mouth, and reduce him to naught by the splendor of his coming."[111] Then, after destroying death itself, he will raise up by the action of the Holy Spirit those who have fallen asleep. And finally, he will hand the kingdom over to his Father, the mystical body having reached its full stature, and God will be everything to everyone and everything.[112] Then will be fulfilled the prophetic oracles: "Death is swallowed up in victory! O Death, where is your victory? O Death, where is your sting?... Thanks be to

111. 2 Thess. 2,1-12.
112. 1 Cor. 15,24-28.

God who gives us the victory through our Lord Jesus Christ."[113]

The Letter to the Hebrews completes this awesome vision. It shows Christ raised higher than the angels and Moses, placed by the Incarnation as mediator between God and man, joined to them in obedience, suffering and death,[114] but free from sin and needing no sacrifice for himself.[115] God has made him, with an oath, the unique and eternal priest;[116] he has invested him with a priesthood more perfect than that of the Old Law, a priesthood prefigured by that of Melchisedec, who was himself superior to Abraham and the levitical priesthood that stemmed from him.[117] As our unique and sovereign priest, Christ has offered but once this sacrifice whose infinite value obtains for men pardon of their sins and an eternal inheritance.[118] Now, dwelling in inaccessible glory, he continues to present his sacrifice to his Father, making continual intercession for us and thus pouring forth on us the merits of his Passion.[119] This intercession of the everlasting priest will last as long as the Church, until the day when he returns in glory to consummate our salvation.[120] It imparts an unwavering strength to the hope held out to us; the author of the Letter compares it strikingly to an anchor for the soul, sure and steadfast, cast as it were up to the very heights of heaven.[121]

The triumphal cries which conclude Paul's eschatalogical passages show him to be a profound optimist, rooted

113. 1 Cor. 15,54-57; cf. Brunot, op. cit., pp. 218-22.
114. Heb. 2,14-18; 5,8.
115. Heb. 4,15-16; 7,26-27.
116. Heb. 5,5-6; 7,20-25.
117. Heb. 7,1-28.
118. Heb. 9,11-29; 10,10.
119. Heb. 6,20; 7,24.
120. Heb. 7,25; 9,24, 28.
121. Heb. 6,19-20.

in the unshakeable foundation of God's power and love which underlies the whole mystery of our Redemption. Nor is this optimism illusory; the Apostle never underestimates the rigorous demands of the combat faced by the Church and each of her members. On the contrary, he provides us with a refreshing example of far-seeing, virile realism; of spiritual vigor and supernatural balance. We have only to follow his example, and we shall never be disheartened or overcome by any obstacle. If we but imitate him, we shall always remain watchful, devoted to our daily work and at the same time venturesome in the service of Christ and radiating hope. By patterning our lives on his, too, we shall come to understand the patience of God and the delays necessary before the world can be converted. We too shall be without illusions and without discouragement. Paul is at the same time one of the greatest mystics, raised on one memorable occasion to the third heaven,[122] and a human being of unusual stature, capable of lofty speculation and profound insight. He was endowed, moreover, with a firm, prudent common sense, as well as an exceptional talent for organization and adaptation. He is aware of the wretchedness of sinful man, as well as of the grandeur of redeemed man; he gave himself up to his apostolic labors[123] out of a consuming love for Christ and his brothers. A far-seeing innovator who refused to make useless and outdated demands, he threw the gates of the Church wide open to pagans even as he remained unwaveringly steadfast, uncompromisingly faithful to the teachings of Christ and the tradition of the other Apostles, which he thinks it impossible to desert without rendering his own work sterile.[124]

It is impossible to repress a feeling of admiration when

122. 2 Cor. 12, 2-4.
123. Cf. Brunot, *op. cit.*, pp. 83-99.
124. Gal. 1,11-12; 2,2; 1 Tim. 6,20; 2 Tim. 1,14; 3,14.

we contemplate this masterpiece of nature and grace. Paul is the fundamental teacher of the Church, the privileged revealer of the mystery of our Redemption,[125] the theologian of both hope and love.

The best way to penetrate his thought is to keep on re-reading his Letters. All the implications of his teaching are not at first apparent, and the various individual passages, which we might judge after one reading to be obscure, help to clarify one another. It is not rare that the comparison of two passages brings out hitherto unnoticed connections; the light as it were suddenly dawns, an ill-understood verse suddenly shines forth with an unforgettable splendor that serves as food for meditation and deepens the spiritual life immeasurably. This action of the Holy Spirit, the primary author of Scripture, will be aided by the reverent interest the reader brings to its study—not only with his mind, but also with his heart, in a sincere desire to apply in his life what he reads. At the same time, he must allow himself to be seized by the force and the gift of sympathy which stream forth from the Apostle. His firmness, his far-reaching demands, his rages are sometimes terrifying; but in spite of all that it is impossible not to love this man, kind and tender even in the midst of his severities, so apparent is it that he never speaks without being moved by an intense love for Christ and for his brothers whom he wishes to save by bringing them to Christ. One stands to gain much from an attempt to achieve a respectful intimacy with Paul and converse with him by reading him, as with a very close friend. The better we get to know him, the more effectively he will cast us into the arms of our divine *Kyrios*, our Lord Jesus, before whom every knee must bend, to whom he devoted his life and for whom he died.

125. Eph. 3,3-9.

Chapter Four

ST. PAUL'S SPIRITUALITY

The Divine Call and Its Demands

Scripture must be read in the spirit in which it was written. It is difficult, therefore, to conceive of a Christian studying St. Paul without adding to his effort to grasp his thought a constant concern for holiness and the apostolate. How, moreover, could the Apostle's invitation to greater union with Christ and uninterrupted spiritual progress possibly leave him unmoved? We shall therefore approach the Pauline Letters now in a spirit of prayer and consider as addressed to ourselves the apostrophe Paul addresses to his correspondents—a bold one, to be sure, but one in which the Apostle'a pride is tempered with profound humility: "Become imitators of me as I am of Christ."[1]

Paul was vividly aware of the call God had addressed to him through Jesus Christ, even as he had done to the prophets of old: "Paul, apostle—not one commissioned by man or by any group of men, but one appointed by Jesus Christ and God the Father who raised him from the dead."[2] God had set him apart even in his mother's womb and called him through his grace to make known his Son.[3] He returns to this point with evident pleasure and gratitude in the

1. 1 Cor. 11,1.
2. Gal. 1,1.
3. Gal. 1,15.

85

salutation of most of his Letters, delighting to call himself an apostle of Christ by God's will.

He lays no less stress, however, on the call to faith of those to whom he writes. The faithful have been called "thanks to the grace of Christ"[4] and in virtue of an eternal choice, prior to the creation of the world, to be holy and without blemish in the eyes of God.[5] There is question here of a loving call to God's adoptive sonship and, in the final analysis, God's Kingdom and glory.[6] The Christian should therefore, like the Apostle, be permeated with the thought of this calling which obviously implies an obligation to be holy: "I...exhort you to conduct yourselves in a manner worthy of the calling to which you have been called, with all humility and meekness."[7]

The divine call implies first of all a renunciation of sin in a true conversion, a complete spiritual reversal. One must turn from idols to serve the living and true God,[8] crucify the flesh with its passionate cravings,[9] despoil and put to death the old, corrupt man and be renewed in the depths of his spirit, and put on the new man created in the image of God[10] so that he becomes in all truth a new creation.[11]

All this cannot be accomplished without painful renunciations; like the Apostle, the Christian is crucified with Christ.[12] With a harsh but necessary candor Paul warns obstinate sinners that they will have no part in the Kingdom

4. Gal. 1,6.
5. Eph. 1,4.
6. Eph. 1,5; 1 Thess. 2,12.
7. Eph. 4,1.
8. 1 Thess. 1,9.
9. Gal. 5,24.
10. Eph. 4,22-24.
11. Gal. 6,15
12. Gal. 2,19.

of God.[13] He himself has renounced not only sin, but all his dignity as a Jew and a Pharisee, all the privileges which he thought were his by reason of his belonging to the Chosen People. He renounced all things to gain Christ. Forgetting what is behind him and directing all his energies toward the future, he hastens straight to his goal to obtain "the prize in store for those who have received from above God's call in Jesus Christ."[14] And he urges his converts to imitate his example, shedding tears over those "who conduct themselves as enemies of the cross of Christ"[15] and do not wish to understand that the scandal and folly of the cross are in fact the highest wisdom[16] and the condition for an eternal reward.

Sharing in the Life of Christ Dead and Risen

But the Cross, although lightened by the fact that it is borne in union with Christ, is only the negative aspect of the Christian life. God has called us in an immeasurable love[17] to live in his love, in a sharing of the divine life. Union with Jesus crucified leads to union with Jesus risen: Christ lives in the Christian, transformed through faith into him who has loved him and delivered himself for him.[18]

These two aspects complement and pervade one another. We live in Christ to the extent that we have died to sin; we must die, but only to be reborn, and we can rise with Christ only if we have first consented to be crucified with him. The stress will be placed now on one aspect, now on the other, according to the individual's state of soul

13. 1 Cor. 6,9-10.
14. Phil. 3,14.
15. Phil. 3,18.
16. Gal. 5,12; 1 Cor. 1,18; 2,6.
17. Eph. 1,5; 2,4.
18. Gal. 2,20.

and the circumstances. But it is only a question of stress: life and death in Christ are inseparable: "If we have died with him, we shall also live with him."[19] "We are heirs indeed of God and joint heirs with Christ, provided, however, we suffer with him that we may also be glorified with him."[20]

These doctrinal and spiritual riches are presupposed in the refrain which St. Paul repeats almost to satiety: *In Christo Jesu*—"In Christ Jesus." This expression is sometimes to be taken in a general enough sense as meaning "from the Christian point of view, in conformity with Christian principles." But most often it must be understood in the strict sense of union with Christ and sharing in his life. The Christian puts on Christ;[21] he lives by faith in the Son of God; Christ lives in him more than he lives in himself.[22] St. Paul considers this idea at length and draws out its implications when he portrays the Christian as predestined to reproduce in himself the image of God's Son[23] and to be intimately united to the various aspects of the redemptive mystery: "When we were dead by reason of our transgressions, he made us live with the life of Christ. By grace you have been saved. Together with Christ Jesus and in him, he raised us up and enthroned us in the heavenly realm."[24]

19. 2 Tim. 2,11.
20. Rom. 8,17.
21. Gal. 3,27.
22. Gal. 2,20.
23. Rom. 8,29.
24. Eph. 2,5-6. In this and several other passages, St. Paul coins compound words by joining the prefix *syn* ("with") to the verbs he uses: die with, be buried with, live with, rise with, be seated in heaven with, be glorified with, etc. This creation of a new vocabulary is deeply significant, for it reveals the forcefulness of our union with Christ — a union so intimate that it could not be expressed in the then-existing Greek language, rich as it was in philosophical and theological terminology.

This transformation is begun in baptism—in baptism into Christ, into his death, his burial and his Resurrection:

> Yes, we were buried in death with him by means of Baptism, in order that, just as Christ was raised from the dead by the glorious power of the Father, so we also may conduct ourselves by a new principle of life. Now since we have grown to be one with him through a death like his, we shall also be one with him by a resurrection like his.[25]

Death to sin must be a state from which there is no turning back, just as physical death is definitive for the body. A relapse into grave sin, which involves the loss of the divine life, should be inconceivable for anyone who has really understood what baptismal grace is:

> Do not then let sin reign in your mortal body so as to obey its lusts. And do not go on offering your members to sin as instruments of iniquity, but once for all dedicate yourselves to God as men that have come to life from the dead, and your members as instruments of holiness for God; for sin shall not have dominion over you, since you are not subjects of the Law but of grace.[26]

The tone is thus set for every Christian's life; it is to be a continuation of his baptismal transformation: "Thus you too must consider yourselves dead to sin, but alive to God in Christ Jesus."[27] And the Apostle outlines this entire spiritual program with characteristic insight:

> But now, set free from sin and become slaves of God, you have your reward in sanctification, which finally leads to life everlasting. For the wages that sin gives is death, but the gift that God bestows is life everlasting in Christ Jesus our Lord.[28]

25. Rom. 6,4-5.
26. Rom. 6,12-14.
27. Rom. 6,11.
28. Rom. 6,22-23.

To sum the whole matter up in one phrase, Christ is "our life."[29] We must be conformed to him; we must, as the French School of the seventeenth century loved to repeat, reproduce in ourselves his "mysteries."

The fecundity of this teaching is obvious, both for a deepening of our spiritual life and for our intimacy with Christ. First of all, we must reproduce our Lord's inner sentiments in ourselves: that humility, obedience, and love which alone gave value to his sacrifice and which reached their most intense expression in his Passion. The sacrifice of Calvary was the most despicable of crimes, from the executioners' viewpoint; but Christ accepted it with complete submission to the command he had received from his Father.[30] Our outward life must obviously differ from his, but we can still imitate him interiorly; we can try to model our obedience on his and thus prolong in ourselves that lovable attitude which more than cancelled the first man's revolt and justified sinners.[31] St. Paul, and with him St. John, thus sets forth a spiritual ideal whose fulfillment transforms a man in the very depths of his being. These two Apostles of love furnish us with a unique goal of ennobling grandeur: loving intimacy with our Lord, whose own love predisposes us to seek him and surrounds us on every side.

St. Paul loves to return to this basic principle of the spiritual life, this perspective of union with Christ dead and risen:

> I would know Christ in the hope that, if I resemble him in death, I may somehow attain to the resurrection from the dead. . . . If, then, you have risen with Christ, seek the things that are above, where Christ is seated at the right hand of God. Set your mind on the things that are above, not on the

29. Col. 3,4.
30. Jn. 10,17-18; 14,31; 15,8.
31. Rom. 5,19.

things that are on earth. For you have died and your life is hidden with Christ in God. When Christ, your life, appears, then you shall appear with him in glory.[32]

Let us observe once again that this twofold task of the Christian is not something optional; it is a strict obligation flowing from his baptismal grace, a vocation to which he must be faithful throughout his life: "Buried with him by baptism, you also rose with him by your faith in the power of God who raised him from the dead."[33]

The Paschal Character of the Christian Life: The Eucharist

It is important to bear in mind that our baptismal rebirth has united us to the paschal mystery. It is a journey, a passage from death to life in union with Christ our Redeemer, which is never finished, never completed as long as we live on this earth. The Apostle stresses this point:

Not that I have already attained this ideal, or have already been made perfect but I press on, hoping that I may lay hold of it, since Christ has laid hold of me. Brothers I do not consider that I have reached it. But one thing I do: forgetting what is past, I strain toward what is ahead. With my eyes fixed on the goal, I press on to the prize in store for those who have received from above God's call in Jesus Christ. All of us, then, who have reached maturity must agree.[34]

The Christian life, therefore, is not a static immobility; and still less, an illusory contentment with what perfection the individual may think he has attained. It must be a continuous Pasch, an uninterrupted effort to attain greater conformity to Christ so as to draw ever closer to "perfect man-

32. Phil. 3,10-11; Col. 3,1-4.
33. Col. 2,12
34. Phil. 3,12-15.

hood, to the mature proportions that befit Christ's complement."[35] By his efforts, which St. Paul compares to the training of track athletes,[36] the Christian must "grow up in every respect in love and bring about union with Christ who is the head."[37] And he must be sustained in this spiritual combat by a well-founded hope of attaining the "crown due to holiness."[38]

This conception of the Christian life should appeal to men of our day, for it is eminently modern. It should furnish strong motivation for, and shed abundant light on, the exhortations to avoid sin and practice virtue which so abound in the "moral" sections of St. Paul's Letters. The analogy of the mystical body, to which we shall return later, is another expression of this same outlook: the members of the body must, if they are not to perish, remain united to the head and live with his life.

The paschal character of the Christian life is again suggested, although not fully spelled out, by St. Paul's teaching on the Eucharist. As a showing forth of our Lord's death until his glorious return,[39] the Eucharist joins us to the mystery of the Passion not only as a memorial of the redemptive sacrifice, but in a wholly present manner—for it is a sharing in the Body and Blood of Christ.[40] It is of course evident that the believer receives, not the dead Christ, but Christ risen and eternally living. Christ is the true paschal lamb,[41] and the reception of his Body and Blood makes us share in his *entire Pasch*, in the total mystery of his being.

We certainly remain wholly within St. Paul's perspective,

35. Eph. 4,13.
36. 1 Cor. 9,24-27.
37. Eph. 4,15.
38. 2 Tim. 4,8.
39. 1 Cor. 11,26.
40. 1 Cor. 10,16.
41. 1 Cor. 5,7.

then, if we look upon the Eucharist as the most effective means we have of growing in the divine life. For as we have seen, Paul himself regards this divine life in us precisely as a sharing in our Lord's Pasch and a prolongation of our own baptismal Pasch. Hence the need for continual progress on our part, since the spiritual life is essentially a *progressive* deepening of the bond joining the members to the head.

Here we see the marvelous unity of the Christian mystery: union with Christ is attained by communion in his *body*. The same body which was nailed to the Cross imparts to us, by reason of our Lord's own institution, a particularly abundant sharing in the graces merited by his sacrifice. Christ, "who was delivered up for our sins, and rose again for our sanctification,"[42] thus gives himself to us, deepening our conformity to him and transforming us more and more perfectly into his own glorious likeness.[43]

Trinitarian Spirituality

Besides its Christocentric character, St. Paul's spirituality also has a marked trinitarian cast. This second aspect completes and perfects the first.

Every single element in the mystery of our Redemption must be traced to the eternal and merciful initiative of our heavenly Father. Even before the foundation of the world, he predestined those he wished to redeem; then, in the fullness of time, he sent his Son into the world to obtain by his sacrifice the forgiveness of our sins.[44] It is he, the Father, who "was truly reconciling the world to himself in Christ, not reckoning against men their sins."[45] And

42. Rom. 4,25.
43. 2 Cor. 3,18.
44. Eph. 1,4; Rom. 3,24.
45. 2 Cor. 5,19.

this action on his part is absolutely gratuitous, the expression of a totally unselfish love.[46] The Redemption is, in fact, the effect of the richness of his grace;[47] we must acknowledge that it is sovereignly free on God's part and unceasingly praise this resplendent grace[48] which has rescued us from the power of darkness and transferred us into the kingdom of God's beloved Son, where our everlasting inheritance[49] now constitutes a dazzling manifestation of the "overflowing riches of his grace."[50]

God's generosity becomes still more overwhelming when we realize its ultimate goal: the gift of adoptive sonship. The Father has in fact "predestined us to be conformed to the image of his Son, so that this Son should be the first-born among many brothers."[51] Here St. Paul casts a new and attractive light on the nature of the Christian life. The gift of grace makes us true children of God, beloved sons of the Father and brothers of Christ, whose redemptive sacrifice has made him the eldest Son in an immense family. And as a result there now exist between the justified man and the divine Persons the closest and most loving bonds. The Father has "predestined us for himself to become through Jesus Christ his adopted children."[52] But whereas human adoption is merely a legal fiction and bestows no new quality on the adopted child, supernatural adoption transforms him interiorly through the gift of the Holy Spirit, the Spirit of the Father and the Son, who remakes him in the Son's image: "And because you are sons,

46. Rom. 3,24.
47. Eph. 1,7.
48. Eph. 1,5-6.
49. Col. 1,13; Eph. 1,18.
50. Eph. 2,7.
51. Rom. 8,29.
52. Eph. 1,5.

God sent the Spirit of his Son into your hearts, crying, 'Abba, Father.' "[53]

This is a profound change from the situation under the Old Law where, although love certainly was not absent, fear was dominant: "Now you have not received a spirit of bondage so that you are again in fear, but you have received a spirit of adoption as sons, in virtue of which we cry, 'Abba, Father.' "[54]

Our heavenly Father, seeing in us the likeness of his own Son, can only regard us as beloved children. When we call him "our Father," therefore, as we recite the prayer Jesus left to the Apostles, our attitude is fully conformed to reality and expresses the most authentic Christian sentiment; it is the Holy Spirit who speaks in us: "The Spirit himself joins his testimony to that of our spirit that we are children of God."[55]

It is with confident assurance that we should say "our Father," but also with profound respect, following in this the example of the Church who, at the end of the canon of the Mass ventures to pronounce the words only in fear and trembling: "We dare to say: our Father...."

In the Christian life, just as in the natural order, important consequences flow from adoption. And here God's generosity surpasses anything the human heart could have imagined:[56] "You are, then, no longer a slave but a son; and if a son, an heir also through God's grace."[57] Again, more precisely still: "But if we are children, we are heirs also: heirs indeed of God and joint heirs with Christ, provided,

---

53. Gal. 4,6.
54. Rom 8,15.
55. Rom. 8,17.
56. 1 Cor. 2,9.
57. Gal. 4,7.

however, we suffer with him that we may also be glorified with him."[58]

But even that is not the whole story. Our inheritance is not merely promised to us; we have already begun here below to possess it in a partial way. The gift of the Holy Spirit (mentioned above in connection with the continuity between the life of grace and that of glory) is its pledge[59] —and the pledge is of the same nature as the entire inheritance. It is not merely a promise, as some translations imply. Our souls are in very truth, then, marked with a seal which imprints on them the divine likeness.[60]

These wonders of God's love create the closest of ties between the Christian and the three divine Persons, so that the Triune God now seems to be infinitely more than a theoretical "dogma" to be "accepted" on faith. His whole life begins to be permeated with dispositions appropriate to the adorable reality: filial obedience toward the Father, brotherly respect and deep intimacy with the Son, and attentive, loving docility toward the Spirit whose temple he has become and whom he must take care not to "extinguish" or "grieve."[61] "Whoever are led by the Spirit of God, they are the sons of God;"[62] through the Spirit who conforms us to the Son we return to the Father whose children we have become. This explains why the Apostle uses the expressions "in Christ" and "in the Spirit" interchangeably when describing our sanctification; since the activity involved is common to both, it can be attributed to either. He even says, elliptically, that the risen Christ is "the spirit"

---

58. Rom. 8,17.
59. 2 Cor. 5,5; Eph. 1,14.
60. 2 Cor. 1,22; Eph. 1,13.
61. 1 Cor. 6,19; 1 Thess. 5,19; Eph. 4,30.
62. Rom. 8,14.

and "a spirit imparting life";[63] for the pouring forth of the Spirit is the fruit of his redemptive sacrifice. But there is no confusion in his thought; he often refers in the same passage to the Father, the Son, and the Spirit in terms which presuppose both their equal dignity and their distinction. He invariably does this, moreover, to stress the Christian's participation in the life of the Trinity:

> There is a distribution of gifts, but the same Spirit distributes them. There is a distribution of ministrations, but it is the same Lord to whom we minister. There is a distribution of activities, but it is the same God who activates them all in everyone.[64]

The call of Jews and pagans to the Faith has united them as one man in Christ and has given all of them "entrance to the Father" by one and the same Spirit.[65] Paul prays that his correspondents may be filled with "the grace of the Lord Jesus Christ, and the love of God (the Father), and the communion of the Holy Spirit.[66] And he extols in lyric terms the wondrous unity which results from these realities:

> There is one body and one Spirit, even as you, from the moment you were called, had the one hope your calling imparted. There is one Lord, one faith, one Baptism, one God and Father of all, who rules all things and pervades all things and sustains all things.[67]

These texts are conclusive; others which affirm the personal character of the Spirit likewise dispel any doubt: the Spirit is sent by the Father;[68] he dwells in the faithful[69] and

63. 2 Cor. 3,17-18; 1 Cor. 15,45.
64. 1 Cor. 12,4-6.
65. Eph. 2,18.
66. 2 Cor. 3,13.
67. Eph. 4,4-5.
68. Gal. 4,6.
69. Rom. 8,9-11.

leads them;[70] he distributes supernatural gifts just as he
wishes;[71] and he presides over the Apostles' work and the
administration of the Church, to the point where it is possible to speak of the gospel of the Holy Spirit.[72]

A *Spirituality of Love*

The Christian's duties and attitudes toward the divine
Persons who dwell in him and whose temple he has become
are summed up in love. Paul himself is an unforgettable
example of this truth, and one from whom we can easily
derive all the inspiration we need.

"I live by faith in the Son of God, who loved me and
sacrificed himself for me[73] —the words are fraught with deep
emotion. Surely no man has understood better than Paul,
the ex-Pharisee, the powerful efficacy of Christ's love. As
he was to write later to the faithful at Rome, thinking no
doubt of himself:

> Why, it is only with difficulty that a person will die to save
> a good man. Yes, it is only for a worthy person that a man
> may, perhaps, have the courage to face death. But God
> proves his love for us, because when we were still sinners,
> Christ died for us.[74]

How conscious he is of Christ's love for him—this Paul
who considers himself unworthy of the name Apostle because he had persecuted the Church of God![75] He places
himself, in all sincerity, "at the head of the list" of the
sinners Christ came to save.[76] He is utterly unable to contain

70. Gal. 5,6 Vg.; Rom. 8,14.
71. 1 Cor. 12,11.
72. Ac. 13,9; 16,6-7;20,22,23-28.
73. Gal. 2,20.
74. Rom. 5,7-8.
75. 1 Cor. 15,9.
76. 1 Tim. 1,15.

his intense gratitude when, at the end of his life, he reflects on Christ's merciful initiative in his regard:

I am grateful to Christ Jesus our Lord, who has strengthened me, because he counted me trustworthy when he made me his minister, although formerly I defamed, persecuted, and insulted him. Still, I obtained the mercy of God because I acted ignorantly in unbelief. Surely the grace of our Lord was lavished superabundantly on me along with faith and the love that results from union with Christ Jesus.[77]

He returns Christ love for love; to this his whole life as an Apostle bears witness. He is a willing slave of Christ and urges the faithful to look on themselves in the same way.[78]

It is out of love for Christ that he endures a difficult imprisonment[79] and suffers innumerable hardships, even to the point of bearing in his own body the marks, or stigmata, of Jesus;[80] he supplies in his own flesh "what is lacking to the sufferings of Christ... for the benefit of his body, which is the Church," of which he has been made a minister.[81]

We carry about with us in our bodies at all times Jesus' condemnation to death, so that in these same bodies of ours the living power of Jesus may become evident. Yes, for the sake of Jesus every moment of our lives we are condemned to death, so that the living power of Jesus may become evident in our weak selves so liable to death. Thus death is at work in us, and life in you.[82]

This crucified and apostolic life, which was to be

77. 1 Tim. 1,12-14.
78. 1 Cor. 7,22-23; Rom. 6,16-19.
79. Eph. 3,1.
80. Gal. 6,17.
81. Col. 1,24-25.
82. 2 Cor. 4,10-12.

crowned by the supreme testimony of martyrdom, has built up the deepest sort of intimacy between Paul and his Savior: "For me to live means Christ."[83] It has created the closest and strongest sort of unity: "He who unites himself to the Lord, forms one spirit with him."[84] But the important thing, from our standpoint, is that he considers the same intimacy and the same unity to be the goal of *every Christian*: "Do you not recognize that Christ Jesus is in you?"[85] It is this overpowering conviction, and not empty rhetoric, that accounts for the Apostle's terrible warning: "If anyone loves not the Lord, let him be accursed."[86]

It is up to each one, then, to show Christ an effective love—not a mere verbal protestation of love, but a love which gladly accepts every sacrifice in union with his Passion. After St. Paul's own example, the Christian must always have Christ's praises on his lips; like him, he must never tire of proclaiming Jesus Savior, Son of God, Lord equal to God, and God himself.[87] And from these acts of faith there must develop a steadfast, selfless love which eventually comes to pervade his entire life.

The Christian's adoptive sonship demands that he requite the Father's gratuitous love. Not that this truth is

---

83. Phil. 1,21.
84. 1 Cor. 6,17.
85. 2 Cor 13,5.
86. 1 Cor. 16,22.
87. St. Paul ordinarily reserves the name "God" for the Father; but he applies it to Christ twice: in Rom 9,5 and Tit. 2,13, although the word *theos* is used in a way quite different, grammatically, from the way it is used when it denotes the Father; see K. Rahner, *Theological Investigations* (tr. C. Ernst, O.P.; Baltimore: Helicon, 1961), pp. 135-38. The other titles Paul gives to Christ presuppose that he is God: he is properly speaking the Son of God (Rom. 8,32) and the sovereign Lord before whom every knee must bend (Phil. 2,11).

completely alien to the Old Testament, since the first commandment of the Law was to love God with one's whole heart, one's whole soul, and one's whole strength;[88] but still, the doctrine of God's fatherhood had not yet been revealed with such clarity. Only the Son, the Father's perfect image,[89] has fully disclosed it; only he has borne witness to the immeasurable love with which the Father delivered his own Son to death[90] and communicated new life to sinners in Christ through the overflowing riches of his grace.[91] It is with a heart filled with loving gratitude that, under the inspiration of the divine Spirit and in Christ who lives in him, the Apostle addresses the everlasting God by the name, Father.[92]

The same primacy of love is evident with regard to the Holy Spirit. Paul, who was to an even greater extent than the prophets of old a man of the Spirit, constantly enlightened and guided by him, portrays the third Person of the Trinity as pre-eminently a "Spirit of love": "God's love is poured forth in our hearts by the Holy Spirit who has been given us."[93] His sensitive and utter docility to the Spirit's enlightenment and inspiration is the reply of his love to the divine love; it shows all those who have received the gift of the Spirit the generosity with which they too must reply to it. The fruit of the Spirit, contrasted with the hateful works of the flesh,[94] makes clear the way we must follow in the practice of love, if we would taste true joy and peace. And God's assurance that he will raise us up on

88. Deut. 6,5; Mt. 22,37-38.
89. Col. 1,15; 2 Cor. 4,4, 6.
90. Rom. 8,32.
91. Eph. 2,5-8.
92. Gal. 4,6; Rom. 8,15.
93. Rom. 5,5.
94. Gal. 5,22-23.

the last day[95] should still further deepen our love for him.

Love is, after all, the last word—the ultimate reality. For "God is love."[96]

The Church, the Mystical Body of Christ

The vocations bestowed by the Holy Spirit are diverse, and so are the gifts by which he enables us to fulfil them. St. Paul mentions several of these gifts on various occasions.[97] He writes to the Corinthians, for example:

> There is a distribution of gifts, but the same Spirit distributes them. There is a distribution of ministrations, but it is the same Lord to whom we minister. There is a distribution of activities, but it is the same God who activates them all in everyone. The manifestation of the Spirit is given to each individual for the common good. For example, to one is imparted the ability to speak with wisdom, to another with knowledge under the guidance of the same Spirit, to another by the same Spirit is imparted wonder-working confidence, to another gifts of healing by the one Spirit, to another the performance of miracles, to another fervent preaching, to another the discernment of spirits, to another the ability to speak in various languages, to another the ability to interpret them. But it is one and the same Spirit who is active in all these gifts, which he distrbutes just as he wishes.[98]

This multiform activity of the Spirit is likened by the Apostle to the functions of the parts of the human body, which in their diversity constitute but one organism:

> Just as the body is a unit, although it has many members, and all the members of the body, many though they are,

95. Rom 8,11.
96. 1 Jn. 4,8, 16.
97. Rom. 12,6-8; Eph. 4,11; 1 Cor. 12,28-30.
98. 1 Cor. 12,4-11.

form but one body, so too is the Christ. In fact, by a single
Spirit all of us, whether Jews or Greeks, slaves or free men,
were introduced into the one body through baptism, and
were all given to drink of a single Spirit.[99]

In his earlier Letters, Paul had expressed a similar idea
when he insisted on the unity of Christians in Christ;[100] here
he gives it greater precision by using the analogy of
the body, a natural comparison which was rather common
in the ancient world. Theologians sum up this teaching
in one phrase when they speak of "the mystical body of
Christ." Although the expression is not Paul's, it conveys
remarkably well the fullness of his teaching; it suggests
both the invisible, interior aspect and the visible, ecclesial
aspect of our union in Christ.

St. Paul used other metaphors to illustrate the same
teaching: e.g., the field,[101] the building,[102] and the marriage
bond.[103] But he has an especial predilection for the analogy
of the body, which he develops with consummate skill in
his First Letter to the Corinthians.[104] Each member of the
human body has its own function, he explains, but the
members are also bound to one another and must work
together for the life of the whole body: "In case one member is in pain, all the members share it. In case one member
is honored, all the members share its satisfaction."[105] Then
he comes quickly to the point: "You are Christ's body and
individually its members."[106] "We, the aggregate, are one

99. 1 Cor. 12,12-13.
100. Gal. 3,28.
101. 1 Cor. 3,6, 9.
102. 1 Cor. 3,9-11; Eph. 2,20-21.
103. Eph. 5,22-33.
104. 1 Cor. 12,14-26.
105. 1 Cor. 12,26.
106. 1 Cor. 12,27.

body in Christ, but individually to one another we stand in the relation of part to part."[107]

There is no question here, although it may so appear at first sight, of a mere moral union such as we might find among the members of a corporation. What St. Paul is talking about is a union with the individual body of the risen Christ: we are the *body* of Christ. This sacred body, the instrument of our Redemption, remains the means whereby the fruits of that Redemption are distributed. Through the Resurrection, Christ's glorious body, inseparable from his Person, has become "a spirit imparting life"[108] —i.e., overflowing with the fullness of the Spirit so as to communicate him to redeemed mankind. The expressions used by the Apostle must be taken in their natural and obvious sense, as referring to Christ's physical body. We are intimately united to this spiritualized and life-giving body by a real union which begins in baptism, by making us members of Christ's dead and risen body,[109] and reaches its climax (as far as this life is concerned) in our reception of Christ's unique Body in the Eucharist.[110] St. Paul teaches the same truth in his Letter to the Colossians, where he explains that in Christ "is embodied and dwells the fullness of the Godhead. In union with him who is the head of every Principality and Power you have been made complete."[111]

Paul always speaks of Christ as a person and as incarnate, never as a moral entity which would include both him and the ensemble of those who believe in him. The communication of Christ's life and the activity of the Holy Spirit

107. Rom. 12,5.
108. 1 Cor. 15,45.
109. Rom. 6,3-11.
110. 1 Cor. 10,16-17.
111. Col. 2,9-10.

which we have discussed above show this clearly; it is obviously a question of union with the individual Jesus Christ. In him dwells all fullness,[112] and through our increasingly intimate union with him he gives us a share in that divine fullness to the extent that this is possible for man.[113] Thus the Christian is called to become as it were a "complementary humanity" for Christ, a continuation of Christ's own human nature.

A new precision becomes clear in the Letters of the Captivity, where Christ is said to act as head and source of life for his mystical body: "He is the head of his body, the Church...Christ is the head of the Church and also the savior of that body."[114]

The members of this mystical organism are alive only because of their union with the head, and they must ever work to deepen that union:

> By professing the truth, let us grow up in every respect in love and bring about union with Christ who is the head. The whole body is dependent on him. Harmoniously joined and knit together, it derives its energy in the measure each part needs only through contact with the source of supply. In this way the body grows and builds itself up through love.[115]

Christ is therefore at the same time the head of the mystical body and the entire body itself, since one cannot become a member of his body without receiving life from him.[116] All the texts we have seen show, moreover, that

---

112. Col. 1,9.
113. Cf. Eph. 3,19.
114. Col. 1,18; Eph. 5,23.
115. Eph. 4,15-16.
116. The same intriguing paradox is found in St. John's Gospel, where our Lord himself says that he is both the Vine and entire plant, including both Vine and branches (Jn. 15,1-7).

Christ's members are at the same time members of one another. Each one enjoys both union with Christ and mutual solidarity with all the others; we are joined not only to the personal Christ, but also to his mystical complement —to all the members of his body to the extent that he communicates himself to them. The individual and collective aspects are inseparable and equally essential. Union with Christ is incumbent on every individual in particular, but the Christian is also a member of a body; our supernatural solidarity is so intimate that no one can be saved or damned in isolation. Everyone is of course bound to work for his own salvation, but he will never achieve it in a separatist, individualistic way.

This character of complementarity is reinforced, in St. Paul, by the identification of Christ's body with the Church. Two texts in particular insist on this identity more than any yet cited.

In showing that the glorified Christ has received from his Father a dignity infinitely superior to that of all the choirs of angels, the Apostle adds: "He has subjected every single thing to his authority and has appointed him as universal head of the Church, which is truly his body, the complement of him who fills all the members with all graces."[117]

The visible Church is therefore properly speaking Christ's body and complement, not in an active way, but insofar as she receives from him the life which permeates his glorified body. It is for the Church that he delivered himself to death with immeasurable love "that he might sanctify her."[118] It is likewise for the Church that the Apostle himself accepts his suffering and hardships: "What is lack-

117. Eph. 1,22-23.
118. Eph. 5,25-26.

ing to the sufferings of Christ I supply in my flesh for the benefit of his body, which is the Church."[119]

From all these considerations two things become easily apparent: first, that the Church is the visible society of the faithful; and second, that her exterior unity exists for the sake of her interior unity, for the sanctification and salvation of each of her members in a sharing of Christ's life. No one ordinarily becomes a part of the mystical body except by joining the Church. Those men who are justified but in good faith do not belong to the Church are members of Christ only in an imperfect way.[120] They have at least an implicit desire to become members in the fullest sense by asking for baptism and joining the visible Church, which will then obtain for them the many graces which she alone has the power to communicate. This twofold unity, exterior and interior, is guaranteed by the gift and activity of the Holy Spirit; it is he who unites the faithful to Christ and to one another in Christ. He is the soul of the mystical body and the Church: "There is one body and one Spirit.... In him you, too, are being fitted by the Spirit into the edifice to become God's dwelling place."[121] "By a single Spirit all of us, whether Jews or Greeks, slaves or free men, were introduced into the one body through baptism."[122]

---

119. Col. 1,24.
120. Fr. Amiot says, in the original, that they are only "potentially" members of Christ's body. This seems difficult to understand; for the justified man shares Christ's life, and membership in his body is precisely a sharing of his life. It seems more accurate to say that such members do not enjoy full, perfect membership in Christ's body until they manifest it outwardly by joining the visible Church and submitting to her discipline. (Tr.)
121. Eph. 4,4; 2,22.
122. 1 Cor. 12,13.

Christian Morality

The doctrine of our union with Christ in his mystical body implies a whole Christian morality, both social and individual in its applications.

Identification with Christ through union with his body and sharing in his life demands that the Christian unceasingly correspond with the grace of his baptism. And this he is to accomplish by making ever more effective, in union with Christ, his death to sin and life for God[123] —by living as an adopted child of God should live. He therefore has a serious obligation to forsake evil and to advance in virtue. But this is not merely a legislative norm with which he must comply by mobilizing his own resources; it is a challenge which he can meet only because he has already received the gift of the Spirit, which enables him to overcome the flesh and conform himself to Christ. It is a challenge which the Savior's intimate presence within him makes welcome and easy. It is, even more accurately, a loving invitation from Christ to prolong in himself the central mysteries of his own Passion and Resurrection.

This unique character of Christian morality, which alone among all the world's moral codes is motivated by love and imparts the very strength needed to fulfil it, is apparent in the duties incumbent on the members of the mystical body. It is because we are all brothers, all one in Christ and closely joined to one another, that each of us must work for the common good by doing his own job as perfectly as possible. Faith, hope, and love[124] —and all the other virtues as well—benefit the whole body at the same time as they perfect the man who practices them. But all of them are

123. Rom. 6,11.
124. Gal 5,5-6; 1 Thess. 5,8.

summed up, for St. Paul, in love, "the bond that perfects,"[125] which is rooted in the love of Christ and without which any actions, even those that seem most heroic, would be worthless: "Follow God's example, as his very dear children, and let your conduct be guided by love, as Christ also loved us and delivered himself for us as an offering to God, a sacrifice that has an agreeable fragrance."[126] Or, more succinctly, "Be of the same mind as Christ Jesus."[127]

Everyone, certainly, is familiar with the eulogy to love which fills the thirteenth chapter of the First Letter to the Corinthians:

> If I should speak the languages of men and of angels, but have no love, I am no more than a noisy gong and a clanging cymbal. And if I should have the gift of inspired utterance, and have the key to all secrets, and master the whole range of knowledge, and if I should have absolute faith so as to be able to move mountains, but have no love, I am nothing. And if I should distribute all I have bit by bit, and should yield my body to the flames, but have no love, it profits me nothing. Love is long-suffering; love is kind, and is not envious, love does not brag; it is not conceited; it is not ill-mannered; it is not self-seeking; it is not irritable, it takes no note of injury; it is not glad when injustice triumphs; it is glad when the truth prevails. Always it is ready to make allowances, always to trust; always to hope, always to be patient.[128]

Love is the fullness, the crowning perfection of the New Law,[129] as it was also of the Old Law if the latter is understood properly. It makes of the Christian a perfectly just man even as it constitutes him a true son of God.

125. Col. 3,4.
126. Eph. 5,1-2.
127. Phil. 2,5.
128. 1 Cor. 13,1-7.
129. Gal. 5,14; 6,2; Rom. 13,8-10.

The practice of love is striking in St. Paul's own life. From the day when Christ's appearance near Damascus made clear the intimate bond joining him to those who believe in him, Paul's heart was filled with a limitless love which will always remain a model for Christians of every age. Rather than multiply citations, let us merely point out the tactful love he lavished so unstintingly on his co-workers, such as Luke, Mark, Titus, and Timothy, and the reverent friendship he bore toward women, whom he associated with him in his apostolic endeavors and whose role he so exalts in the new world-order he helped to form. With regard to one of them he has left us this delightful confidence: "Greet Rufus, the elect in the Lord, and her who is his mother and mine."[130]

Paul considers himself both father and mother to those he has evangelized:[131] on the one hand, they are his "dear children," for whom he endures the pains of childbirth until Christ is formed in them;[132] and on the other hand, he glories with all humility in his spiritual fatherhood: "Although you may have a thousand guides in Christ, you have but one father, myself, who by preaching the Good News to you begot you in Christ.[133]

Even when he must reprimand the recalcitrant Corinthians, he still protests his love: "But I will most gladly spend myself and be spent to the limit for the sake of your souls, even though the more I love you the less I am loved."[134]

This is a love which excludes no one; not a day passes but Paul is obsessed with concern for all the churches:

130. Rom. 16,13. Conf.
131. 1 Thess. 2,7.
132. Gal. 4,19.
133. 1 Cor. 4,15.
134. 2 Cor. 12,15.

"Who is weak without my sympathizing with his weakness? Who is led astray without my burning with indignation?"[135]

He is saddened by the unbelief of his countrymen, for whose sake he would gladly be separated from Christ if that could help them.[136] He lavishes as much attention on a poor slave he has begotten while in chains as on the master, Philemon, whom he begs to welcome him as a beloved brother.[137] He becomes

> a Jew to the Jews to win over the Jews; to those subject to the Law, a man subject to the Law (though not myself subject to the Law), to win over those subject to the Law; to those not having the Law, a man not having the Law (though I am not without a law, since I am subject to the law of Christ), to win over those that have not the Law. I become like a weak man for the weak to win over the weak. I become all things to all men, by all means to win over some of them.[138]

He is, in brief, a living image of his Master, who died for all men. There is no need, surely, to stress the pertinence of this apostolic outlook for our own time.

Thanksgiving, Joy, and Peace

It is hardly surprising that so exalted a spiritual outlook should culminate in a habitual attitude of thanksgiving, joy, and peace.

Deeply and painfully aware as St. Paul is of sin and its ever-present evils, the thought of our Lord's redemptive sacrifice and the countless blessings it has brought fills him with an unshakeable confidence. For he has grasped, as few other men have done, that *Christ's triumph over sin*

135. 2 Cor. 11,28-29.
136. Rom. 9,3.
137. Philem. 10-16
138. 1 Cor. 9,20-22.

and death guarantees a similar victory for those who believe in him![139] Small wonder that his attitude is invariably one of thanksgiving. Small wonder that he begins virtually every one of his Letters by thanking God for the faith and other supernatural gifts his correspondents have received, even as he assures them of his continued prayers for them. These passages are like a leit-motiv of joy in which he asks his brothers to join:

> Always be joyful. Never cease praying. Always be grateful. Such sentiments God wills you to have in Christ Jesus. . . . Give thanks to God the Father everywhere for every gift in the name of our Lord Jesus Christ. . . . Whatever you do or say, let it always be in the name of the Lord Jesus, while you give thanks to God the Father through him.[140]

This is a valuable and ever-pertinent lesson which the Church implements by placing expressions of gratitude at the heart of her most solemn prayers, especially the Mass, whose very name, "Eucharist," means "act of thanksgiving." We are, unfortunately, only too prone to forget to thank God. Ever eager to multiply our requests, we seldom bother to acknowledge God's goodness in granting them. We would do well, then, to take to heart Paul's advice, to let our petitions be made known to God "by prayer and supplication *with thanksgiving.*"[141]

Gratitude for God's blessings gives rise to a supernatural joy which persists even in the midst of suffering. Here again, St. Paul is our example. He is overflowing with joy, he says, despite all his troubles;[142] and he expects a similar joy to characterize all the faithful: "Rejoice in the Lord

139. 1 Cor. 15,57.
140. 1 Thess. 5,18; Eph. 5,20; Col. 3,17.
141. Phil. 4,6; emphasis added.
142. 2 Cor. 7,4.

always; I repeat, rejoice...Always be joyful."[143]

Christian joy is like the flower of a sacrifice bravely borne; it rewards generosity of effort even as it stimulates to further holiness. A work joyfully done is always more perfect than a task grudgingly performed: "God loves a cheerful giver."[144]

Joyful service of the Lord establishes a man firmly in that deep, abiding peace which God alone can give: "Then the peace of God which surpasses all understanding will guard your hearts and your thoughts in Christ Jesus."[145]

Letting the peace of God pervade our whole life makes it possible for us to live at peace with other men; and conversely, if we behave peaceably toward others, the God of peace will dwell more fully and effectively in us: "Be comforted, live in harmony, be at peace; and the God who is the source of peace and love will be with you."[146]

The Christian who is true to his calling is an effective builder of peace because he is first at peace with God, and this is perhaps the most important message St. Paul has for our broken world. Before it is too late, we must learn that Christ is our peace[147] —that Christ calls all men to salvation and unites them in one body, quickened by the Holy Spirit and permeated with love.[148] Spiritual peace among men enlivened by the same faith is the best guarantee we have of temporal peace:

> But all over these virtues clothe yourselves with love; it is the bond that perfects and binds them together. Let the

143. Phil. 4,4; 1 Thess. 5,16.
144. 2 Cor. 9,7.
145. Phil. 4,7; cf. Jn. 14,27: "Peace is my legacy to you: my own peace is my gift to you. My giving to you is not like the world's way of giving."
146. 2 Cor. 13,11.
147. Cf. Col. 1,19-20.
148. Eph. 2,11-22.

ruling principle of our hearts be the peace of Christ, to which you were called as members of one body.[149]

When the Apostle begins each of his Letters by wishing us grace and peace from God our Father and the Lord Jesus Christ, he expresses the best and most effective of greetings, for he is fully aware that our spiritual combat "holds promise for the present life as well as for the next."[150]

The Eternal Perspective

As the reader has no doubt noticed, every element of St. Paul's spirituality has, besides its significance for our Christian life here below, an eternal perspective. Baptism, to begin with, gives a share in the life of the risen Christ. This new life then brings about a moral resurrection within us, which becomes final and irrevocable at the moment of death. And finally, if we accept death as Christ did on the Cross, then by a supreme paradox death will itself be, for us as for him, the gateway to everlasting happiness:

> If, then, you have risen with Christ, seek the things that are above, where Christ is seated at the right hand of God. Set your mind on the things that are above, not on the things that are on earth. For you have died and your life is hidden with Christ in God. When Christ, your life, appears, then you shall appear with him in glory.[151]

The truth emerges once again from these considerations that Christian morality is strictly dependent on the doctrine of union with Christ and with the other members of his body. This doctrinal basis confers on it an impressive sublimity and an uncompromising strictness, but it also makes it attractive and easy to observe. The Christian is not told

149. Col. 3,14-15.
150. 1 Tim. 4,8.
151. Col. 3,1-4.

to obey rigid, arbitrary laws under pain of damnation; he is only invited to manifest outwardly the deep-seated inner transformation he has already undergone in his baptism. He is invited to give external testimony of his death to sin and his new life for God in Christ. This is in itself a magnificent and ennobling ideal held out to the Christian, but it is still further enhanced by the glorious and unending consummation promised him if he achieves it. Not only will the faithful Christian always be with Christ,[152] but his body, as the instrument by which he performed his good works, will be raised up on the last day under the quickening action of the Holy Spirit.[153] As a result, glorified in both soul and body, he will enjoy an everlasting destiny fully conformed to that of the Lord Jesus. How, then, can he ever lose heart in the spiritual combat which will lead him "to perfect manhood, to the mature proportions that befit Christ's complement?"[154]

Then, when the redemptive mystery is complete and the mystical body has reached its full stature, Christ will hand over to his God and Father the Kingdom he has purchased with his own blood.[155] God will be everything to everyone and everything,[156] and his glory, the ultimate goal of all the divine actions throughout history, will be perfectly manifest.

"All things belong to you...the world, or life, or death; or the present, or the future. All things belong to you, and you to Christ and Christ to God."[157] The Father has chosen us before the creation of the world, predestined us to be-

152. 1 Thess. 4,17.
153. Rom. 8,11.
154. Eph. 4,13.
155. Cf. Apoc. 19,1.1-16.
156. 1 Cor. 15,24-28.
157. 1 Cor. 3,21-23.

come his adopted children through Jesus Christ, and marked us with the seal of the Holy Spirit, only, in the final analysis, to the praise of his resplendent grace and glory.[158] It could not be otherwise, as every mystic—Elizabeth of the Trinity, for instance—has clearly perceived. The utter disinterestedness, continual preoccupation with God's Kingdom, and burning desire for God's glory which are implied in these Pauline texts should inspire and crown the outlook of the Christian. Like Jesus Christ, into whom he has been literally incorporated, he too should come to live only for the glory of his Father.

This is the ultimate lesson taught us by the Apostle, the central point at the heart of his spirituality which dominates and perfects all its other aspects.

158. Eph. 1,4-14.

BIBLIOGRAPHY

This work is not a scientific treatise, but an introduction to the personality and thought of St. Paul. The following bibliography reflects this character of the work as a whole; it is designed mainly to call attention to other books which, while they are also popular or semi-popular in nature, develop in greater detail aspects of St. Paul's temperament and doctrine which have been briefly presented here. The listing does, however, include some deeper, more technical studies in which some readers may be interested; the most scholarly of these have been marked with an asterisk.[1]

I.   *Latin and Greek Text:*
     Augustinus Merk, S. J. *Novum Testamentum Graece et Latine.* 7th ed. Rome: Biblical Institute, 1951.

II. *Annotated English Translations of the Bible:*
     James A. Kleist, S.J., and Joseph L. Lilly, C.M. *The New Testament.* Milwaukee: Bruce, 1954. This version, generally held to be the best now available in English, has been used throughout the present

---

1. The French bibliography in the original edition has been entirely replaced by an English one more useful to the new audience to which this translation is addressed. It seems important to point out, however, that the reader who knows French or Latin will derive great benefit from consulting the standard commentaries of Fathers Lagrange, Huby, Knabenbauer, etc. (Tr.)

translation, except for Rom. 8:3-4 and 16:13, taken from the Confraternity translation.

Ronald A. Knox. *The Holy Bible*. New York: Sheed and Ward, 1956. Perhaps the most readable, and certainly the most elegant translation yet produced, this version is so free that it occasionally departs slightly from the precise meaning of St. Paul.

Confraternity of Christian Doctrine. *The New Testament*. Paterson: St. Anthony Guild, 1941. This translation, eventually to be replaced with a more modern one, is extremely literal in its adherence to the Vulgate text.

III.   *Lives of St. Paul:*

Igino Giordani. *St. Paul, Apostle and Martyr*. tr. C. Maranzana and M. Williamson. New York: Macmillan, 1946.

Joseph Holzner. *Paul of Tarsus*. tr. F.C. Eckhoff. St. Louis: Herder, 1945.

Henri Metzger. *St. Paul's Journeys in the Greek Orient*. tr. S.H. Hooke. New York: Philosophical Library, 1955.

Giuseppe Ricciotti. *Paul the Apostle*. tr. A. I. Zizzamia. Milwaukee: Bruce, 1952.

Albert C. Williams. *Paul, the World's First Missionary*. New York: Association Press, 1954.

IV.   *Commentaries on the Letters:*

New Testament Reading Guide. Collegeville: Liturgical Press, 1952. A series of fourteen inexpensive pamphlets which embody the latest insights of contemporary biblical scholarship in concise, easily understood form. Numbers 6-11 are on St. Paul's letters, and the first of these contains an excellent introduction to St. Paul.

Herbert N. Bate. *A Guide to the Epistles of St. Paul*.

New York: Longmans, Green, 1956.

Charles J. Callan, O.P. *The Epistles of St. Paul.* New York: Wagner, 1922. 2 vols.

Ronald A. Knox and Ronald Cox. *It Is Paul Who Writes.* New York: Sheed and Ward, 1959. Contains the full text of the Knox translation with commentary on pages facing the text.

J. MacEvilly, D.D. *Exposition of the Epistles of St. Paul.* 7th ed. Dublin: Gill, 1910. 2 vols.

A. Robert and A. Tricot. *Guide to the Bible.* tr. E.P. Arbez, S.S. 2nd ed. New York: Desclee, 1962. 2 vols. The commentary on St. Paul's Letters is in the first volume.

A *Catholic Commentary on Holy Scripture.* London: Nelson, 1953. Besides the commentary on the individual Letters, which is somewhat out of date despite the recent date of publication, there are separate articles dealing with New Testament history and theology.

V. *Doctrinal and Spiritual Studies:*

Paul, Trumpet of the Spirit. (ed. Sr. E.J. Daly; an anthology). Paterson: St. Anthony Guild, 1963. A collection of first rate, authoritative contributions covering many facets of St. Paul's personality and thought.

Francois Amiot. *Key Concepts of St. Paul.* tr. J. Dingle. New York: Herder and Herder, 1962.

*Lucien Cerfaux. *Christ in the Theology of St. Paul.* tr. G. Webb and A. Walker. New York: Herder and Herder, 1959. The standard work on this subject.

*———. The Church in the Theology of St. Paul. New York: Herder and Herder, 1960.

William J. McGarry. *Paul and the Crucified.* New

York: America Press, 1944.

Vincent P. McCorry. *Everyman's St. Paul*. New York: Farrar, Strauss, 1961.

Jacques Maritain. *The Living Thought of St. Paul*. tr. H.L. Binsse. New York: Longmans Green, 1941.

*George T. Montague. *Growth in Christ*. Kirkwood, Mo.: Maryhurst Press, 1960.

*Fernand Prat, S.J. *The Theology of St. Paul*. tr. J.L. Stoddard. Westminster: Newman, 1950. 2 vols. Formerly the standard work on Pauline Theology, it still retains its place as a classic in the field and has still to be supplemented by newer works in several areas of study.

Robert Sencourt. *St. Paul, Envoy of Grace*. New York: Sheed and Ward, 1948.

W. David Stacey. *The Pauline View of Man*. London: Macmillan, 1956.

*David M. Stanley, S.J. *The Resurrection in Pauline Soteriology*. Rome: Biblical Institute, 1961.

Claude Tresmontant. *St. Paul and the Mystery of Christ*. tr. D. Attwater. New York: Harper, 1957.

Alfred Wilkenhauser. *Pauline Mysticism*. tr. J. Cunningham. New York: Herder and Herder, 1960.